Flora Thompson's Country

View of the countryside at Shelswell Park, home of Flora's Thompson's squire, Sir Timothy.

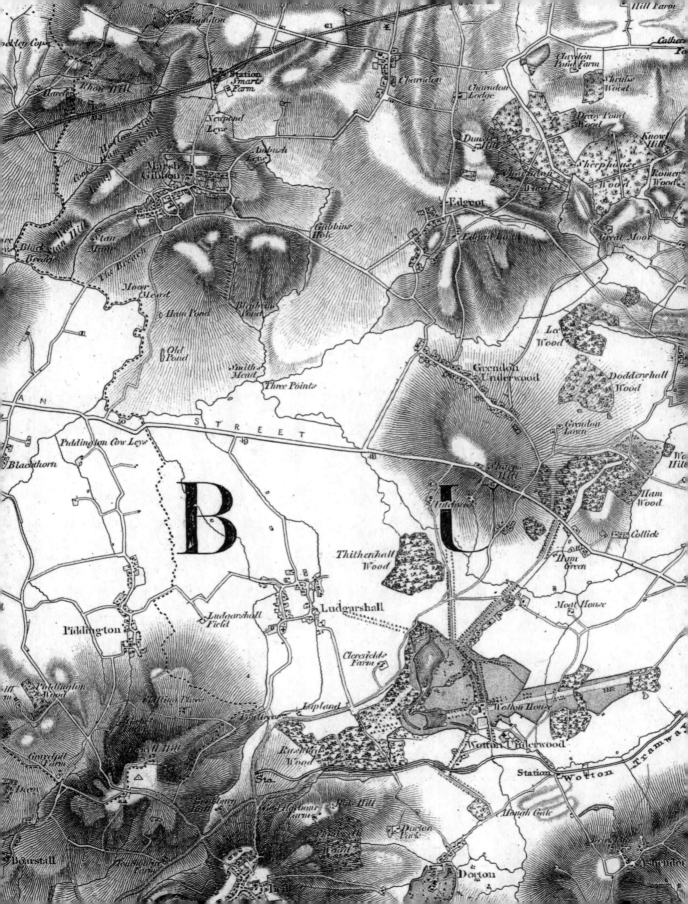

Front cover shows the Forge and Post Office at Fringford where Flora Thompson
worked for Mrs Whitton.
(Courtesy of William Plumb)

Front map showing villages in the vicinity of Bicester.
Scale: one inch to a statute mile
Printed from an Electrotype made in 1887
Published at the Tower of London 1 October 1833 by Lieutenant Colonel
Colby of the Royal Engineers
Engraved at the Ordnance Map Office in the Tower under the direction of
Lieutenant Colonel Colby by Benjamin Baker and Assistants
The writing by Eben.r Bourne
(Courtesy of the Centre for Buckinghamshire Studies)

Rear map showing villages in the vicinity of Brackley and Buckingham
Scale: one inch to a statute mile
Printed from an Electrotype made in 1891
Railways inserted to July 1890
Published at the Tower of London 1 October 1833 by Lieutenant Colby of the
Royal Engineers
Engraved at the Ordnance Map Office in the Tower under the direction of
Lieutenant Colonel Colby by Benjamin Baker and Assistants
(Courtesy of the Centre for Buckinghamshire Studies)

Back cover shows members of Form Four at Marsh Gibbon School in 1897. On the
left, stands teacher Helena Bowden, and on the right, her husband, head
teacher Henry Bowden, aged forty-five. Both Mr and Mrs Bowden were
certified teachers from Reading. Mr Bowden acted as the enumerator for the
1891 census for Marsh Gibbon.

FLORA THOMPSON'S COUNTRY

The Real Villages and Towns of
Lark Rise to Candleford

David Watts
and
Christine Bloxham

Robert Boyd
PUBLICATIONS

Published by
Robert Boyd Publications
260 Colwell Drive
Witney, Oxfordshire OX28 5LW

First published 2009
reprinted 2011

ISBN: 978 1899536 96 2

Printed and bound in China,
produced by Lion Production, Hong Kong

Contents

Flora Thompson photographed in a hand-knitted woollen jumper with tassels in the late 1890s. The photographer has captured the essence of her reserved personality and shy disposition. (Courtesy of Henry Westbury)

Acknowledgements

We would particularly like to thank the following people and institutions who have generously provided information and assistance with photographs:

Mrs Margaret Adams (Stoke Lyne), Gordon Allen (Cottisford and Tusmore), Banbury Museum, Ernest Bagwell (Chetwode), Colonel Anthony Barkas (Tusmore), Peter Barrington (Bicester), Mrs Beth Baughan (Piddington), Mrs Mary Bryden and Mrs Pat Tucker of the Launton Historical Society (Launton), Buckinghamshire Museum (Boarstall and Buckingham), Sid Castle (Launton), The Centre for Buckinghamshire Studies (Boarstall, Buckingham and Marsh Gibbon), The Centre for Oxfordshire Studies (Banbury), Mrs Eileen Chambers (Marsh Gibbon), Miss Evelyn Clayton (Bicester), Norman Coward (Bicester), The Revd Philip Derbyshire, Associate Priest in Buckingham Benefice (Buckingham), Miss Dorothy Dew (Alchester and Bicester), Mrs Edith and Edwin Faulkner (Ludgershall), Harold French (Stoke Lyne), Mrs Marian Doris Goble (Stratton Audley), Mrs Bertha Green (Blackthorn), Arthur Goss (Stratton Audley), Miss Connie Harris (Bicester), Martin and Heather Haslett (Boarstall, Brackley, Cottisford, Fringford, Hethe, Marsh Gibbon, Piddington and Stratton Audley), Rowland and Steven Herring (Blackthorn), John Hill (Bicester and Middleton Stoney), Peter Hoare (Ludgershall), John Hollis (Ambrosden), Phillip and Margaret Hudson (Bicester and Stratton Audley), William Hudson (Bicester), John Jackson (Ardley and Launton), Miss Elfreda Jones (Ambrosden and Blackthorn), Mrs Hilda Jones, (Piddington), Brian and Eva Judge (Marsh Gibbon), John Kiely (Launton), Mrs Joan Kirby (Middleton Stoney), Mrs Audrey Lambert (Bicester, Buckingham, Launton and Piddington), Baroness Von Maltzahn (Shelswell), David Markham (Blackthorn), Michael Morgan and his father the late William Harris Morgan (Bicester and Middleton Stoney), Jean and David Morris (Juniper Hill), Miss Dorothy Mountain (Bicester), The Oxfordshire Museum, Woodstock (Ardley), Mr and Mrs Patrick Phillips of Kentwell Hall, Suffolk (Bicester), Bill and Beryl Plumb (Fringford and Stoke Lyne), Mrs Rene Prentice (Bucknell), Len Rees (Blackthorn and Boarstall), The Rice family (Marsh Gibbon), Wafic Said (Tusmore), Fred Smith (Bicester), Tony and Iris Tallents (Piddington), Mrs Eira Waine (Ambrosden and Blackthorn), Herbert Waine (Bicester and Launton), Leslie Wallington (Ludgershall), Tony Webster and the Trustees of the Old Gaol Museum Buckingham, Henry Westbury (Juniper and Souldern), Miss Nellie Waddup (Marsh Gibbon).

We would also like to thank our families for their patience, particularly Molly Watts and Norman Blanks, Dorothy Bainton for her encouragement of the project, and our publisher Robert Boyd for his professional expertise and patience in bringing the publication of this book to fruition. Lastly, we would like to thank Roger Bettridge, for his patience and skill in proof-reading the manuscript.

The Rise, Juniper.

The allotments, Juniper.

Introduction

Flora Thompson was born in 1876 in the otherwise unremarkable North Oxfordshire hamlet of Juniper Hill, on the northern fringes of the county, just south of Brackley, rechristened *Lark Rise* in her inimitable trilogy *Lark Rise to Candleford*, which contains such an evocative description of the rigours of life in the late Victorian countryside. She was a truly remarkable writer, as she came from a working-class background (although as revealed later in the book, she can trace her roots back to notable and wealthy ancestors such as the Lambournes and the Becks). She was born the daughter of a stonemason, Albert Timms, who himself came from yeoman farmer stock, and a nursemaid, Emma Dibber. Although her parents were marginally better off than her agricultural labourer neighbours, they lived in a small cottage with few luxuries and it was always a struggle, if not to make ends meet, then to achieve any level of comfort.

Flora herself was a shy child, an onlooker rather than a participator, and this perhaps is the secret of her art. A participator sees largely one aspect of an event, whereas an onlooker can take in the wider picture. Flora's genius is that she was able to retain a clear picture of the way of life of her youth (which encompassed a turning point in life in the rural community, when machines were taking the place of labourers in the fields and there was a mass exodus to the industrial towns) and describe it from the point of view of her middle age, so that she was able to put it into perspective and comment on the hardships endured and the changes. She also included many small details of domestic life such as cooking methods and descriptions of interiors which are seldom found elsewhere. She was writing from the stance of someone who had lived the life, whereas most people writing about the countryside were writing from a middle-class perspective, and could not appreciate the nuances as Flora could. She emphasizes the hardships of the life lived by the agricultural labourers, who were the backbone of the countryside. Her characters are based on the people she grew up with and in many cases they can be traced back to the actual people, although she has made a few changes, perhaps to protect their anonymity, perhaps because she thought of herself as writing a novel, although it is in fact her thinly disguised autobiography.

In describing Juniper Hill (*Lark Rise*), her own village, and Cottisford (*Fordlow*), where she went to school, she has been largely accurate, but when venturing farther afield she has combined experiences of different places in different parts of the country. Flora worked at the Fringford Post Office and Forge for Mrs Whitton (whose character but not physical appearance is seen in *Miss Lane*), but she wrote that *Candleford Green* was not meant to represent Fringford accurately (although it certainly does in depicting the forge and Post Office) and there are definite echoes of Bicester. Flora has few direct references to her town of *Candleford*, but wrote that it was based on Banbury and Buckingham, and it almost certainly contains elements of Brackley and Bicester too.

Lark Rise to Candleford was originally published in three volumes by Oxford University Press: *Lark Rise* in 1939, *Over to Candleford* in 1941 and *Candleford Green* in 1943. It was most unusual for the Press to publish such works, as they did not publish fiction. Sir Humphrey Milford, the publisher, was immensely proud of having published her work and considered *Lark Rise to Candleford* one of the two most important works published during his twenty-two years at the Press, along with Arnold Toynbee's *A Study of History*. Flora continued her thinly veiled autobiography in *Heatherley*, which describes her stay in Grayshott, on the Surrey-Hampshire border, and wrote another novel, *Still Glides the Stream*, set in Oxfordshire. In later life she wrote nature notes for the *Catholic Fireside*, some of which have been published in *The Country Calendar*, edited by Margaret Lane, and *The Peverel Papers*.

Further details of Flora's characters and places can be found in Christine Bloxham's book *The World of Flora Thompson Revisited*, and Gillian Lindsay has written her biography in *Flora Thompson: The Lark Rise Writer*, while more of Bicester's past is described in the series *The Changing Faces of Bicester* by David Watts and Peter Barrington. The Old Gaol Museum in Buckingham has recognised her work by creating a permanent display about her and building up a collection of her works and memorabilia as a study centre. Her writing has struck such a strong chord that not only is her work still in print over sixty years after her death, and published in many languages, but it has been brought to new audiences by the BBC dramatisation, although this is only loosely based on her actual writing.

Flora would have known many of the villages described in this book very well and a look at their history takes us back to her more distant roots, which she herself never knew about, tracing her ancestry back to the middle ages and showing how a simple Victorian country girl could claim to be related to aristocracy and how deeply her family's history is interwoven with that of the Bicester area and the wider world.

This book seeks to unravel some of the strands of Flora's history and illustrate aspects of the rural way of life she would have known such as the agriculture and rural crafts which characterised the area. Many of Flora's relations farmed locally or were involved in crafts such as wheelwrighting.

It also delves into aspects of the fascinating and diverse history of the villages of the Bicester area and the towns – Buckingham, Banbury and Brackley – which combine to make Flora's *Candleford*, each of which has its own unique character.

BOARSTALL

Although Boarstall is situated just over the county border in Buckinghamshire, it has close links with Oxfordshire and with the royal medieval hunting forest of Bernwood.

The village is dominated by Boarstall Tower and its highest population was 255 inhabitants recorded in 1861. Owing to its proximity to Otmoor it was referred to in the rhyme relating to the 19th-century enclosure riots:

> *I went to Noke*
> *But nobody spoke,*
> *I went to Beckley*
> *They spoke directly,*
> *Boarstall and Brill*
> *They are talking still.*

According to legend, Nigel, an Anglo-Saxon huntsman, single-handedly killed a large and savage wild boar which was spoiling King Edward the Confessor's hunting, allegedly by putting a sow into a pit to entrap the boar, where he decapitated it, presenting the king with the creature's head impaled on his sword. Edward rewarded him by presenting him with an area of land called Derehyde at Boarstall, which he held on 'horn tenure.'

The medieval history of Boarstall is closely linked to Bernwood, as the medieval manor house, of which Boarstall Tower, now owned by the National Trust, is the sole remains, was built for Nigel's successors, who served as forsters of the forest. The manor was owned by several families, the FitzNigels losing it briefly after the Norman Conquest, but it was returned to them and descended via the female line to John de Handlo who married Joan Fitz Nigel. He was given licence to crenellate the manor house in 1312 and built a defensive moat around it. His daughter, Elizabeth de Handlo married Edmund de la Pole, Knight Banneret of Kingston-upon-Hull, whose family became one of the most prestigious in the land. In the 15th century the house was owned by the wealthy Rede family, and it was during their tenure that the Boarstall Cartulary was assembled, recording documents connected with the property from 1170 to 1499; it includes the oldest coloured map depicting an English village.

The house emerged unscathed from the Wars of the Roses, but played a bigger role during the Civil War, changing hands several times as it was in a strategic position near the Thame to Oxford road. It was initially garrisoned by Parliament but in 1644 Thomas Gage took it for the Royalists. The widowed Penelope, Lady Dynham, née Wenman, who supported the Parliamentarians, had to submit to Royalist occupation. During the siege of 1645

Lord Fairfax reputedly lost 300 of his 1200 men during one day when Boarstall Tower was strenuously defended by Sir William Campion, who had only about 100 men. The house only fell when Campion heard that Oxford, the King's headquarters, had fallen.

In the late 17th century the house descended to the Aubrey family of Llantrithyd in South Wales. We have a glimpse of the house from the catalogue of the sale of the household furnishings of Sir Thomas Aubrey, Baronet, in 1769, in which the rooms are listed, including bedrooms for servants over the bakehouse and larder, nursery, red, yellow and green bedrooms, six other bedrooms, breakfasting room, best chamber galley (complete with billiard table), tapestry room, best parlour, hall, common parlour (with card table), butler's pantry, servants' hall, kitchen, brewhouse, dairy cellar, wash-house and laundry, stables, kennel, barn, etc.

Tragedy struck the Aubrey family when John, the six-year-old son and heir of Sir John Aubrey (1739-1826), Sixth Baronet of Llantrithyd, and his wife Mary Colebrooke died suddenly, allegedly from 'eating contaminated gruel', which may have contained a fungus causing ergot, which can be fatal. An alternative version suggests that Sir John had been instructed by his wife to give their son some medicine and administered it from the wrong bottle, despite his son's remonstrations that it was the wrong one. At the time some thought that the death was caused by witchcraft. Soon after the Aubrey family moved to Dorton House and Boarstall Manor house was demolished apart from the tower. Mary died four years later and was buried by her son.

Boarstall is also famous for its 17th century duck decoy, probably built by Sir John Aubrey and today in the care of the National Trust. It is one of only three remaining in working condition in England. It was designed to attract large numbers of wildfowl to the two and a half acre lake using fake decoy ducks to attract them into long cones of wickerwork and netting forming a tunnel (known as a pipe) where they could be easily caught. As they were not shot, pellets did not have to be removed before eating, so they attracted higher prices.

Flora Thompson's great-uncle Edward Wallington lived at Chilling Place, the 14th century farmhouse on the side of nearby Muswell Hill, in the 1830s. The house was described in a 1912 sale catalogue, now in the Centre for Buckinghamshire Studies, as:

An exceptionally fine 14th century Manor House most pleasantly situated on an eminence about 370 feet above Sea Level, commanding fine and extensive views over a large tract of Country. It contains: Entrance Hall, Dining Room, 27ft. 6in. by 11ft; Small Parlour, Drawing Room, 18ft. by 16 ft. 3 in.; Having fine old oak panelled walls and beautifully carved cornices and oak overmantel, Large kitchen fitted with open fireplace, washing furnace, pump and cupboards, dairy 27ft. by 14 ft. 6 in. churn house, pantry, coal house, two underground cellars, five good and spacious bedrooms (two of which have fireplaces), and three attic bedrooms over. In front is the kitchen garden, orchard and paddock … The Water Supply is from a never-failing well.

The farm also boasted various farm buildings and must have been a desirable residence. Its location on Muswell Hill is interesting as it has been suggested that the earthwork at the top of the hill may have been a horticultural maze.

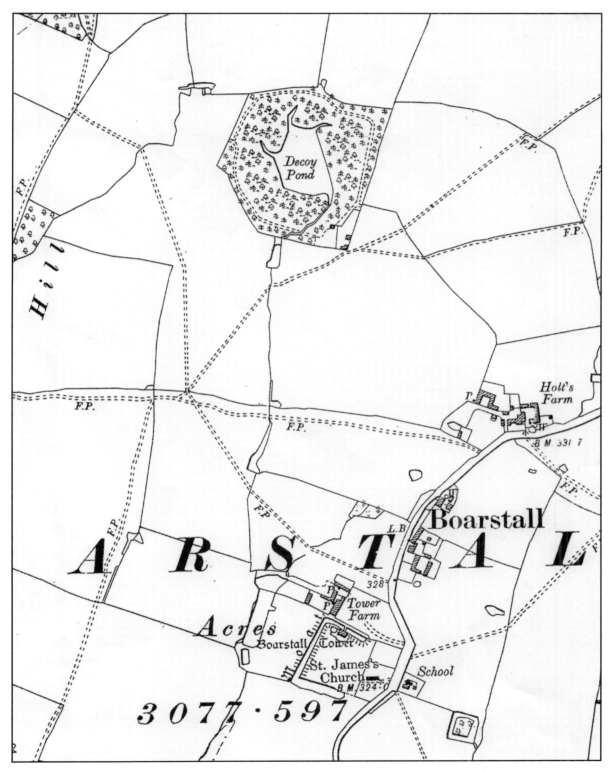

Ordnance Survey map of Boarstall showing the village, tower and decoy in 1900.

Plan of Boarstall in the mid 1440s featured in the *Boarstall Cartulary,* which was made for Sir Edmund Rede of Boarstall House (1413-1489) and may have been shown to King Henry VI on his visit to Boarstall in c1444. Reproduced from Lipscomb's *History of Buckinghamshire* (1847).

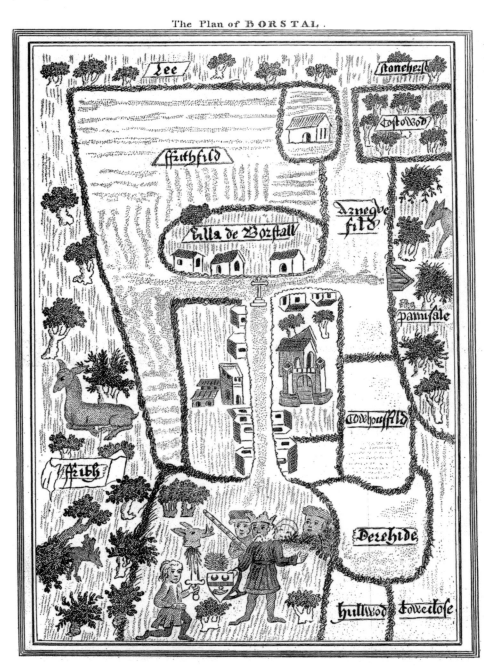

At the bottom of the map Sir Edmund's ancestor Nigel the Forester is shown presenting Edward the Confessor with the head of a ferocious boar which had terrorised the Bernwood forest. In the centre Sir Edmund's great fortified gatehouse is clearly visible immediately west of the village street of Boarstall, which is headed by a preaching cross. On the right a wooden gate gave access to the Panshill district of the Bernwood Forest. It is believed to be the oldest map of a village in England.

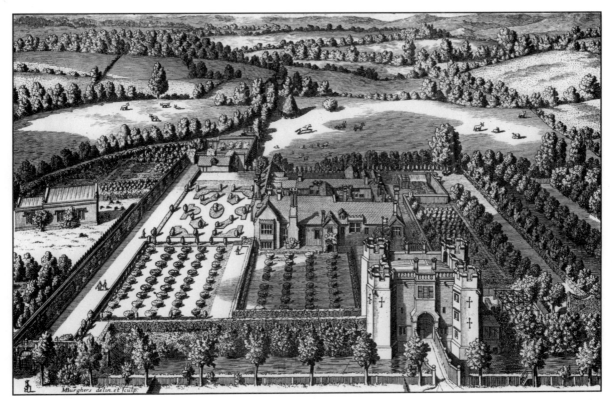

Boarstall keep-gatehouse and mansion, etched and engraved by Michael Burghers, in *The Parochial Antiquities attempted in the History of Ambrosden, Burcester, etc*, (1695) by White Kennett, Vicar of Ambrosden. The mansion house seen in the middle foreground behind the gatehouse survived the Parliamentary artillery bombardment mounted between 1644 and 1646. The house was eventually pulled down in about 1778 after the accidental poisoning and death of John Aubrey, junior, aged 6, in Boarstall house in 1777.

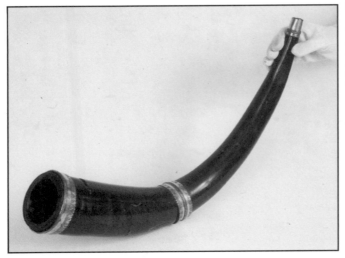

The Boarstall Horn presented to Nigel the Forester as his symbol of office as Keeper of the Bernwood Forest on behalf of the King. While the bison or buffalo's horn itself may date from the 12th century (compare the Savernake Horn), the silver mounts are dated on stylistic grounds to the mid 15th century, so it is possible that the horn was specially made for Sir Edmund Rede at the time of the compilation of the Boarstall Cartulary. (Courtesy of the Centre for Buckinghamshire Studies)

A sculpture of the ferocious wild boar which is alleged to have been killed by Nigel the Forester and was wrongly believed to have given Boarstall its present name.

The front of the keep-gatehouse at Boarstall viewed from the north. The building was constructed by Sir John de Handlo, who received a licence to crenellate and wall his existing moated manor house in 1312. Sir John was a former constable of St Brivaels Castle in the Forest of Dean. The stone bridge seen here replaced a wooden drawbridge which was operated from a chamber immediately above the gate arch. The large upper room on the second floor above the drawbridge chamber comfortably seats over one hundred people and may have been intended for meetings of the Forest court.

Boarstall Tower viewed from the south-east. The two doorways at the base of the turrets immediately left and right of the gatehouse arch give access to two newel staircases leading to the drawbridge chamber and roof.

The foundations of a 17th century brick oven found near the southern section of the moat during the 2008 excavations of the house at Boarstall Tower.

One of two Bellarmine jars recovered from the moat of Boarstall Tower near the main gate during dredging operations carried out in 1955. The jar was given to the actress Ena Burrell, a tenant of the Tower who frequently entertained well-known guests such as Sir Laurence Olivier and his second wife Vivien Leigh. The jar dates from the time of the Civil War and carries a caricature of the face of Cardinal Robert Bellarmine (1542-1621), a Catholic theologian who opposed the reformed church and was a leader of the Counter Reformation. Bellarmine jars were often used as witch bottles and contained potions, iron pins, nails and even human hair to thwart a witch's curse. Frequently they were hidden in house walls near the main doorway or around a major fireplace. (Courtesy of Martin Haslett)

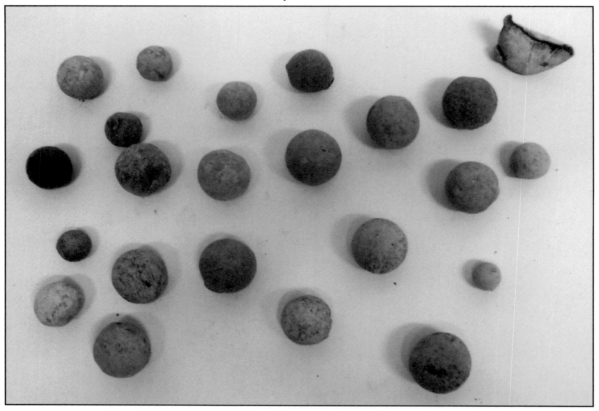

A collection of twenty-two musket balls fired from the pallisaded ramparts of Boarstall House against parliamentary forces who laid siege on at least three occasions between 1644 and 1646 with considerable loss of life. The small lead container, top right, is a measure for priming a musket with gunpowder. (Courtesy of Martin Haslett)

The Decoy lake at Boarstall, which covers two acres and still feeds the moat around the Tower with water. The Decoy has four 'pipes' into which ducks were driven and trapped. (Courtesy of Martin Haslett)

Entrance to a decoy pipe showing a dog at work with the ducks following him, drawn by Sir Ralph Payne-Gallwey (illustration from *The Book of Duck Decoys* by Sir Ralph Payne-Gall-wey, Bt., 1886).

Close-up view of the netted pipe which lies adjacent to the Keeper's cottage at the Boarstall decoy. (Courtesy of Martin Haslett)

Here Daniel White (1843-1929), one of the longest-serving keepers of the Duck Decoy at Boarstall, is standing next to a screen alongside one of the water channels (known as pipes) at the Decoy in 1923. He was born at Wotton Underwood, the son of Joseph White, a gamekeeper, and his wife, Ann. He worked for the Aubrey-Fletcher family as both Decoy keeper and gamekeeper and lived with his family in the cottage next to the Decoy from 1870 until his death. Daniel left effects valued at £223. (Courtesy of Buckinghamshire County Museum)

The Decoy keeper's cottage at Boarstall. The earliest part of the house appears to have been built of locally-made red brick in the 1830s /40s and is shown as a modest rectangular structure on the 1851 tithe map (C.B.S. Tithe Map 50, Diocesan copy). A northern extension appears to have been added prior to 1880, when the first edition of the Ordnance Survey 25 inch map was published. The map shows the house with its present 'L'-shaped ground plan.

Muswell Hill viewed from the Boarstall Duck Decoy. The side of the hill directly overlooking Boarstall still has the remains of two artillery platforms which supported cannon used by Parliamentary forces for the bombardment of Boarstall House in the three sieges staged between 1644 and 1646. There were three farms on the hill, one of which, Muswell Hill farm, on the summit, was farmed by James Shaw, dairyman, while another nearby, known since the early 17th century as Chilling Place, was the home of Edward Wallington (1808-1877) and his daughters, who married into the Sulston family. Edward Wallington was the eldest brother of Martha Wallington, Flora's grandmother, while James Shaw was a great-great-uncle of Flora Thompson. (Courtesy of Martin Haslett)

Chilling Place farmhouse on the side of Muswell Hill in 1911. Flora Thompson's great-uncle Edward Wallington lived here in the 1830s, and her cousins, the Sulstons, were still resident in the 1870s. The house is said to date back to the 14th century and the deeds record various owners of the property back to 1546. Chilling Place covers some three hundred and twenty-nine acres and lies half in the parish of Piddington and half in Brill. Two of the fields are still known as Sulston's big meadow and Sulston's little meadow and cover sixteen and four acres respectively. Other fields have the interesting names of Badgers' Spinney, Banky Piece, Upper Sweethill, Ploughed Hare Hill and Hare Hill meadow.

The area in front of New Park Farmhouse, Panshill, Boarstall. This was the site of one of the most famous prize-fights held in England in the 19th century, fought between John Broome and Jack Hannan on 26 January 1841. The fight took place on the Oxfordshire / Buckinghamshire county boundary running through New Park farm, so that the spectators could escape 'across the border' if the police suddenly arrived. The actual location was kept a secret as long as possible to thwart possible police intervention. The police were successfully lulled into thinking that the fight would take place near Brackley. News of the fight travelled fast and thousands of spectators arrived from London and Birmingham, via Aylesbury and Bicester. The fight lasted forty-seven rounds but after Hannan dislocated his wrist Broome was declared the winner. An interesting account of events surrounding the fight was recorded by J. K. Fowler, the licensee of the *White Hart* inn in Aylesbury in his book *Echoes of Old Country Life*. In this he wrote:

> *'Some amusing episodes occurred that day. One friend of mine, a leading farmer in the neighbourhood of Bicester, attended the fight on horseback, and some men, who were pressed upon by his horse, earnestly entreated him to take charge of a poor little boy, about twelve years old, who they said, was being nearly crushed to death. My friend kindly permitted them to put the lad up behind his saddle; he told the boy to put his arms around him and to hold on tight. The boy did so, and when near the close of the fight, the men heartily thanked my friend for his kindness … and lifting the innocent little lad down, were soon lost sight of. The rider then discovered his watch and purse were gone, and every farthing he had, nearly £20.'*

Fowler recorded that on the same day thieves attending the fight stole £100 in plate from the King's Arms in Bicester and all the takings from the Bulls Head and the Crown Inn in Aylesbury.

Drawing showing the celebrated fight between the prize-fighters Broome and Hannan for a prize of £1000.

LUDGERSHALL

Ludgershall is another Buckinghamshire village on the fringes of Bernwood Forest. Kingswood, a hamlet of the village, has a legendary connection with Henry II, as it is said that he had a bower here where he would visit his mistress 'Fair Rosamund', and a local track is known as *Rosamunds Waye*. This has echoes of Rosamund's Bower at Woodstock Palace.

The village is Anglo-Saxon in origin and a curious story links it with Edward the Confessor. Wulwin Spillecorn, a Saxon yeoman's son from Ludgershall, lost his sight after sleeping in the sun for too long while resting after felling timber. He remained blind for seventeen years, then dreamed that he should visit King Edward, who would restore his sight. He duly travelled to the royal court and gained an audience at which he related his story to the King, who dipped his hand in water and touched Wulwin's eyelids: blood dripped from his eyes, his sight was restored and Edward granted him charge of the Palace of Windsor.

In the Domesday Book of 1086 Ludgershall, then named *Litlegarsele*, was held by the Bishop of Coutances. Henry II granted three hides of land and an acre of wood to the Brethren of the Holy Trinity of St Inglevert in Picardy and a hospital was to be built on the land, although it is not certain whether this was ever done.

The advowson to the church was owned by the Knights Hospitallers from the mid 13th century until the Dissolution. Although there was a church here in the 13th century, and probably much earlier, most of the present church dates from the 14th and 15th centuries. Sir John de Handlo, who held Boarstall, also held Ludgershall in the mid 14th century.

A famous medieval incumbent of the church was the theologian John Wycliffe, founder of the Lollard movement, who was rector here from 12 November 1368 until about 1390. He was presented by John Pawley, Prior of the Hospital of St John of Jerusalem in England, and may have lived in a chamber on the first floor of the medieval church porch. He was able to retain his close links with Oxford University and used his influence to try to reform the church, railing against the excesses of its wealth and wanting to return to the teachings of the scriptures. He was instrumental in translating the Bible into English.

Flora Thompson has a connection with Ludgershall as her Wallington and Lambourne ancestors lived here for generations and many of their names are recorded in the parish registers. The Wallingtons moved to Ludgershall from Worminghall in c1590. The burial of William Wallington, juvenile, is recorded on 7 March 1591 and there are many Wallington gravestones in the churchyard. Perhaps the most famous member of the family was Nehemiah Wallington, a turner of Cheapside, London, who was descended from the Botolph Claydon branch of the family. He was brought up before the Court of Star Chamber in 1638, charged with issuing seditious Puritan tracts, and his diary (which is preserved in the Guild-hall Library) gives a detailed account of his interrogation plus eyewitness accounts of the businesses on London Bridge and details about plague victims.

The marriage of Edward Wallington, Flora's great-great-grandfather, was by special licence:

> *May 15 1770. Which day personally appear'd Edward Wallington of Ludgershall in ye county of Bucks Farmer and a Batchelor aged nineteen years and alleged that he intended to marry with Clemence Lamborn of Ludgershall aforesaid in ye Archdeaconry of Bucks spinster aged twenty three years having Parents' consent and not knowing or believing any Impediment to hinder ye said intended marriage.*
>
> *Of ye truth of ye. . . Premises he made Oath and pray'd Licence for them to be married in ye Parish Church of Ludgershall aforesaid in ye Archdeaconry aforesaid.*
>
> *Sworn before Fra. Greesley ...   Edward Wallington*

The Lambourne family, who were yeoman farmers, moved to Ludgershall from Twyford and the churchyard contains the gravestones of Elizabeth, née Kent, who married John Lambourne at Drayton Parslow in 1702, and her husband John Lambourne, who died in December 1741.

Ludgershall was enclosed relatively early in 1777, when the lord of the manor was Sir John Borlase Warren, and, as shown in the 1851 census, the chief occupation was agriculture, with 25 farmers and one bailiff, over 100 agricultural labourers, two waggoners, one shepherd, one cowherd and one gamekeeper, the latter in Kingswood. The craftsmen generally supported agriculture, such as the carpenters and blacksmith. Other craftsmen such as cordwainers probably made boots and shoes for the villagers, while the frock maker was probably making agricultural smocks rather than dresses. Most of the female villagers – nearly 70 of them - were lacemakers, but only four were fifteen or younger, the youngest being twelve, suggesting that the industry was already in decline. A dressmaker and milliner and a pedlar are also found.

Shops included two butchers, a grocer, a general stores and three beer shops. The 79-year-old parish clerk and sexton William Jones was also a pauper and many of the elderly people were described as paupers. In 1851 the principal residents were Thomas Martyn, the Rector, who was 58, and schoolmaster John Matthews, aged 35, and his eighteen-year-old wife Emma, who was the schoolmistress. The National School had been founded four years earlier in 1847. After enclosure Mrs Martyn, widow of John Martyn, who had been Professor of Botany at Cambridge University, purchased the lordship of the manor and several of her descendants were presented as vicars there.

The village has several houses with 17th century origins and maps reveal traces of medieval fishponds and a moated site near the church. A recent excavation to the north of the village revealed remains of a 15th century pottery and tile industry in the Brill and Boarstall tradition.

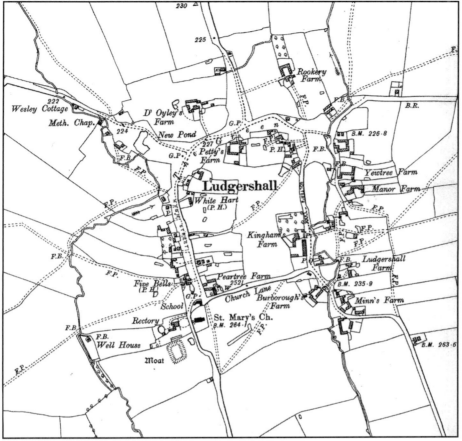

Ordnance Survey map showing the village of Ludgershall in 1900.

Part of a bird's-eye view of the remains of Bernwood Forest showing Ludgershall from the east, drawn between 1564 and 1587 and believed to have been made for the Goodwin Court Case. Ludgershall is clearly shown with its main axis orientated north-south and the parish church situated at the south end of the village. The general street layout has not changed dramatically since this view was drawn. In the foreground to the left of the Wotton Underwood windmill can be seen the giant oak tree which was felled by Flora's ancestor John Beck of Woodham in 1600. (Courtesy of the Huntington Library, California)

Ludgershall High Street looking north in 1900. Most of the houses set back from the street are hidden by giant elm trees since killed by Dutch Elm disease in the 1970s. The disease effectively destroyed more than 99% of the elms in southern England within a few years and completely changed the visual appearance of the landscape of Ludgershall and that of the neighbouring villages.

Members of the Ludgershall Friendly Society assembled outside Ludgershall village school at the southern end of the High Street on 31 May 1900. Most of the local villages had their own friendly societies e.g. Piddington, Blackthorn, Marsh Gibbon, Fringford, Hethe and Stoke Lyne. Marsh Gibbon had two societies operating in the 19th century.

Ludgershall Church, Brill, Thame.

Ludgershall church in the early 1900s. The names of numerous members of Flora Thompson's Wallington and Lambourne ancestors are recorded in the parish registers as having been baptised, married and buried there. One of the earliest Wallington family entries in the registers is that of William Wallington, juvenile, who was buried on 7 March 1591.

The porch of Ludgershall church. In the photograph Edwin Faulkner is showing John and Molly Watts the gravestones of John and Elizabeth Lambourne, who were two of Flora Thompson's direct Lambourne ancestors. John Lambourne and his wife Elizabeth, appear to have died within a few days of each other in December 1741. The chamber over the ground floor of the porch may have been used by the theologian John Wycliffe when he visited Ludgershall from Oxford to officiate at services. John Wycliffe entered into the rectorship of Ludgershall on 12 November 1368 and continued in the post until 1390 or later.

Capital in the south aisle of Ludgershall church. The capitals decorated with cowled figures with interlocked arms are believed to have been carved by a local stonemason. Similar late 13th/early 14th century work, possibly by the same sculptor, is found at Bloxham, Fringford and Hampton Poyle churches.

A picturesque view of a group of thatched barns and farm buildings in 1905 situated in the vicinity of the Green, Ludgershall. (Courtesy of the Centre for Buckinghamshire Studies)

Part of the Ludgershall cow common in front of the *Bull and Butcher* public house in 1903. It was one of three public houses which once existed in Ludgershall, the others being the *White Hart* and the *Five Bells*. Licensing records suggest that the *Bull and Butcher* was first licensed as a public house in 1805, when the licensee was Henry Harris. Between 1764 and 1828, the two licensees of the *White Hart* in the High Street were Christopher and John Lambourne, who were members of Flora Thompson's Ludgershall Lambourne family. (Courtesy of the Centre for Buckinghamshire Studies)

The Green, Ludgershall, c1910. On the left can be seen the *Bull and Butcher* and on the extreme right is the 18th century home of the Wallington family, which has had a side range demolished and is now much reduced in size.

The home of Flora Thompson's Wallington ancestors in Ludgershall. The Wallington family moved into the village in c1590, having previously lived at Worminghall and Stratton Audley. Perhaps the most well-known member of the family was Nehemiah Wallington (1598-1658), the turner of Cheapside, who was descended from the Botolph Claydon branch of the family.

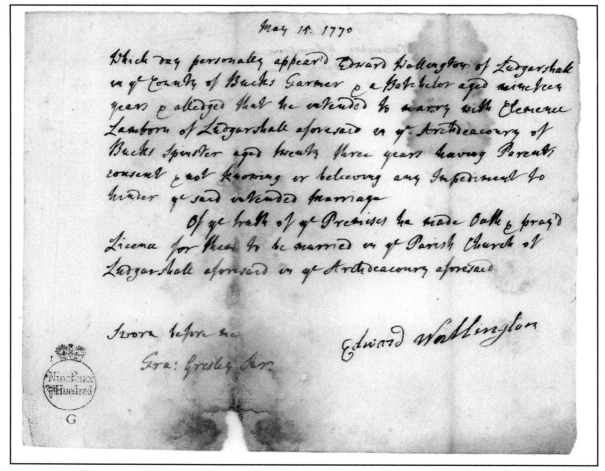

Marriage licence allegation for the marriage of Edward Wallington and Clemence Lamborn which took place in Ludgershall in 1770. (Courtesy of the Centre for Buckinghamshire Studies)

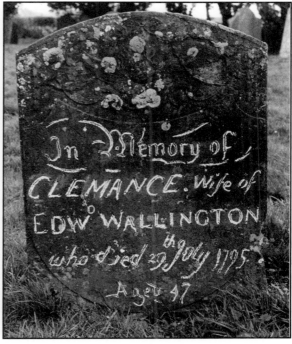

Left: Gravestone in Ludgershall churchyard to the memory of Edward Wallington, yeoman, who died on 17 April 1808 in his fifty-eighth year. Edward was born and baptised at Ludgershall in 1750, the youngest son of Thomas Wallington, yeoman, and his wife Mary Hine. Edward Wallington and his wife Clemence/Clementina Lambourne were the great-great-grandparents of Flora Thompson. Right: Gravestone marking the grave of Clemence Wallington, née Lambourne, the wife of Edward Wallington, who died on 29 July 1795 at the comparatively young age of forty seven.

Leslie Wallington standing in his living-room in Holly Cottage in Ludgershall High Street in 1990. Mr Wallington, who was born in 1914, was a distant cousin of Flora Thompson. The thatched cottage now has brick walls but may have started life as a single-storied half-timbered medieval structure.

Wayside Cottage on the northern edge of Ludgershall village. The cottage lay adjacent to twenty acres of arable land and was the family homestead of the Lambourne family through-out much of the 18th century. A branch of the Lambourne family later moved from here to Rookery Farm in the fields opposite. Ludgershall tradition has it that loot taken by the local highwayman in the late 18th century was stashed away at Rookery Farm. In 1908 Richard Lambourne moved from Rookery Farm to the Ramblers, Ludgershall.

Richard Lambourne (1843-1917) with his wife Jane (1833-1921) and daughter Ellen (1877-1922) outside the Ramblers.

Edwin Faulkner of Ludgershall Farm, another distant cousin of Flora Thompson. Mr Faulkner's father, Thomas, used to graze up to ten cows on the twenty-one acres of common in the centre of Ludgershall village. In the 1920s the cows were supervised by a boy cow-keeper who frequently left the cows to wander and cause havoc in villagers' gardens. The practice of grazing cows on the village 'cow' common was eventually abandoned due to the widespread damage the cows caused.

One of Mr Faulkner's cows grazing on the Green in the centre of Ludgershall village in the 1920s.

PIDDINGTON

Piddington existed before the Norman Conquest and in 1152 the manor was granted by Simon de Senlis to St Frideswide's monastery in Oxford, later reverting to the Crown. Like Boarstall it was later owned by the Aubrey family.

Piddington has a close connection with Flora Thompson as her Shaw and Wallington ancestors lived here. The Shaws moved to Piddington from Islip in the late 1680s and before that lived near Shipton-under-Wychwood. John Shaw, a wealthy yeoman farmer like his ancestors (many of whom left substantial wills), built *Brown's Piece* in the 18th century and lived here with his wife Elizabeth Beck, whom he married by licence in 1781. Their only surviving child Martha inherited the farm, which was run by her husband Edward Wallington, who came from Ludgershall, and it was here that Flora's grandmother Martha Wallington was born. *Brown's Piece* is situated in the centre of the village at the junction with Arncott Road. The farm consisted of a house and garden, an orchard, barn, stables and yard, rickyard, cow house and yard, paddock, pasture and arable land.

Flora and her father Albert Timms would have been fascinated to know about their Beck ancestry, as Albert was immensely proud of being descended from yeoman stock and the Becks held high offices of state. The Beck family had a lordship at Eresby in Lincolnshire in the 12th century and lived at Doddershall, Buckinghamshire, in the early 14th century. Several members served as royal tax collectors and one was Abbot of Thame. A branch of the Eresby family, known as de la Beche, lived at Aldworth in Berkshire and their funeral effigies rank as some of the best surviving from the 14th century. One of the effigies is that of Sir Nicholas de la Beche or Becke, who was tutor to the Black Prince and Constable of the Tower of London. In 1337 he was granted lordship of the manor of Piddington for service to the king, although he only held it for a short time, in turn granting it to Sir John Sutton, Lord of Dudley. He fought at the Battle of Crécy and was awarded the post of Seneschal in Gascony, dying around 1348. John Beck of Bicester, a direct ancestor of Flora Thompson, set up a charity in his P.C.C. will in 1675, leaving land in Waddesdon for the apprenticeship of poor boys from Woodham, Westcott and Waddesdon. His wife Ann Delafield was descended from William Delafield, who died in 1404 and was believed to have acted as steward of the Waddesdon Manor estate for the Black Prince.

The farm owned by Martha Shaw and Edward Wallington did not prosper so in 1805 the couple borrowed £700 from Martha's aunt Elizabeth Shaw to buy more stock, putting the farm up as collateral. By 1815 they owed her £1647 10s, so the ownership of the farm passed to Elizabeth, with the proviso that the Wallingtons could have it back on repayment of the loan. Elizabeth died in 1820, leaving the farm to Martha (pointedly not to Edward) for her lifetime, stating that after Martha's death it was to be divided between her children. Edward was to have no say in running the farm. Flora Thompson wrote in a letter to Mrs

Oldacre in 1921 that *'Drink, gambling and utter recklessness has brought my grandfather (also of fairly good family) down to poverty'* and was probably referring here to her great-grandfather Edward Wallington. In 1824 disaster struck the family: Martha, aged only 40, and three of her children, fourteen-year-old Francis, six-year-old Edwin and seventeen-year-old John died and were buried between the beginning of March and 17 May. A year later Edward Wallington died, aged 44, and the remaining children became orphans: Edward was only seventeen, Elizabeth thirteen, Leonard twelve, Martha eight and Clementina three. None of their immediate relatives seemed to be prepared to take care of them, two uncles claiming that they could not do so because they were in 'indifferent circumstances' themselves, so the children muddled on as best they could. Events came to a head in 1829 when Edward wanted to marry Mary Sulston, so the financial situation was clarified in a very Dickensian way by taking it to the Court of Chancery. The only way the financial tangle could be sorted out was to sell the farm, which was purchased by Revd John Cleobury of Piddington for £900, and Thomas Stevens, a yeoman of Piddington, was made formal guardian to the children. Money was paid to clear outstanding bills to various local tradesmen and for school fees and the remaining money was divided between the children: Edward received £109 2s, Leonard had only £7 16s 6d after his apprenticeship to a cabinet maker had been paid, Elizabeth received £105 14s 2d, Martha £79 4s 11¾d and Clementina £95 1s 8¾d.

Another inhabitant of Piddington, also descended from the Beck family and therefore distantly related to Flora Thompson, was John Drinkwater (1882-1937), who described the village in *Inheritance, being the first book of an autobiography*, p. 47:

It is a plain, grey little village… ambling from cottage to cottage with no apparent sense of direction, its half dozen larger houses of red brick sitting discreetly here and there at the roadside … When I knew it, a stranger was seen only when one passed through in the carrier's cart, or when the Irish labourers came over for hay harvest … In the winter, when icicles were on the thatch eaves, the village would lie for days as if it were asleep.

Drinkwater wrote a poem describing the ghost seen at the Blackthorn toll gate in a poem published in *Seeds of Time* in 1921:

> *The toll-gate's gone, but still stands lone,*
> *In the dip of the hill, the house of stone,*
> *And over the roof in the branching pine*
> *The great owl sits in the white moonshine.*
> *An old man lives, and lonely, there,*
> *His windows yet on the crossroads stare,*
> *And on Michaelmas night in all the years*
> *A galloping far and faint he hears …*
> *His casement open wide he flings*
> *With 'Who goes there?' and a lantern swings.*
> *But never more in the dim moonbeam*
> *Than a cloak and a plume and the silver gleam*
> *Of passing spurs in the night can he see,*
> *For the toll gate's gone and the road is free.*

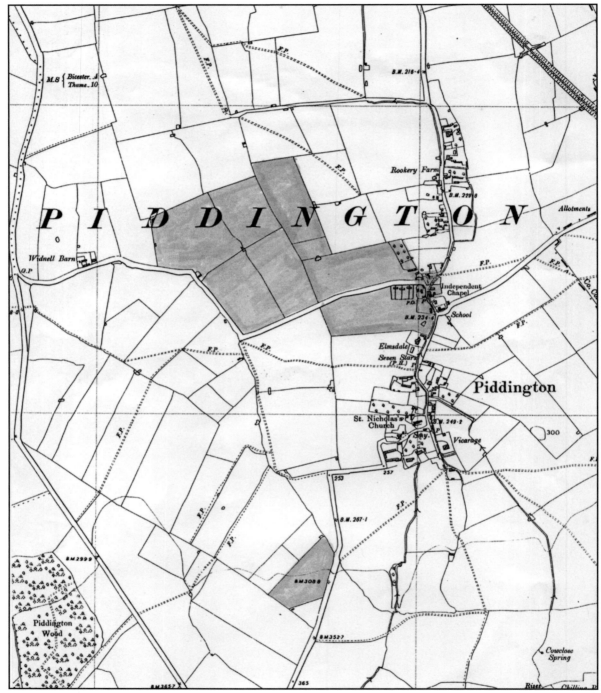

Ordnance Survey map of Piddington published in 1900, showing the land-holding farmed by Flora Thompson's great-grandparents Edward and Martha Wallington at the centre of the village. The farm, originally owned by Martha's father John Shaw, became the subject of the Wallington Court case heard in the Court of Chancery in 1829 and 1830.

The Hermitage on the side of Muswell Hill overlooking Piddington, drawn by E. Williams and etched by J. and H.S. Storer in 1822. Bicester's local historian John Dunkin records that the site was given in 1092 by Guido de Ryale and his wife Joan de Piddington to Ralph, a hermit, who built a hermitage and a chapel dedicated to the Holy Cross. *The Hermitage* seen here was built on the site of the original 11th century hermitage.

Piddington church, where many of Flora Thompson's Shaw and Wallington ancestors were baptised, married and buried. Jennifer Sherwood describes the chancel (c1300) as being unexpectedly sumptuous with interesting graduated lancet windows and a sedilia, piscina and Easter sepulchre, all elaborately carved. The nave is 13th century and is plain by the standards of the chancel. The low west tower is held to be 16th century. The church contains a faded picture of St Christopher, probably painted in the 14th century. (J. Sherwood and N. Pevsner *The Buildings of England, Oxfordshire*, 1974, p. 731).

The burial ground of many of Flora Thompson's Shaw ancestors, immediately outside the south porch of Piddington church. The gravestones represent four generations of the Shaw family, the earliest surviving stone being that of John Shaw (1691-1767), yeoman, Flora's great- great-great-grandfather. Several members of the family were wealthy yeoman farmers who left substantial Archdeaconry and Prerogative Court of Canterbury wills.

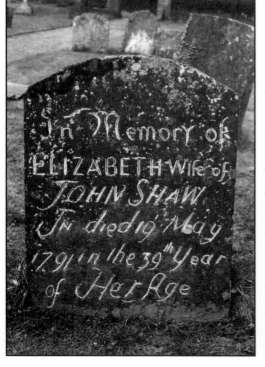

The gravestone of Elizabeth Shaw, née Beck (1762 – 1791), in the Shaw burial ground. Elizabeth was the first wife of John Shaw, yeoman, of Brown's Piece, Piddington, and married him at Piddington in 1781. They had one surviving child Martha (born 1784), who married Edward Wallington by licence at Ludgershall in 1805. Elizabeth Beck's family can be traced back to Eresby in Lincolnshire where the family had a substantial lordship in the 12th century. Flora's direct Beck ancestors arrived at Doddershall, Buckinghamshire, in the early 14th century. (Note: the stone was chalked in over over 30 years ago and is now indecipherable. The 3 in 39th year is actually a 2).

The effigy of Sir Nicholas de la Beche in Aldworth church, Berkshire, showing him wearing leather body armour sewn down the sides of the chest. His head is covered by a close-fitting leather helmet, which in turn rests on a heavy metal helmet turned sideways.

Sir Nicholas's face has a moustache and his hands are clasped in prayer.

Cottages at the end of Vicarage Lane in a quiet corner of Piddington near Manor Farm on a hot summer's day in the early 1900s. One of the properties has been demolished to make way for a bungalow, but the other house still remains.

Piddington Vicarage in c1905, which originally belonged to Flora Thompson's great-great-uncle James Shaw, dairyman, of Muswell Hill. James Shaw exchanged the house for another in a special arrangement with the church in the last year of his life.

Manor Farm, Piddington, the home of John Drinkwater's great-uncle, yeoman farmer Thomas Brown. John Drinkwater, the poet and dramatist (fourth cousin of Flora Thompson), lived with his grandfather John Beck Brown, ironmonger, in north Oxford and spent most of his summer holidays as a child and youth at Piddington. According to John Drinkwater in his autobiographies *Inheritance* and *Discovery* (1931 and 1932), four of Thomas Brown's sons were farmers: Tom farmed at Woodeaton, John at Elsfield and later Marsh Gibbon, Arthur at Boarstall and Charles had farms at Piddington and Launton. A fifth son Albert was a banker. According to John Drinkwater, Charles and Arthur were notable members of the Bicester Hunt and received gifts of cuff-links made of gold-mounted fox teeth from Lord Valentia, the Master of the Hunt, which were held to be a mark of great distinction.

Pencil and ink study of John Drinkwater by the artist E. H. Rennington drawn in 1917.

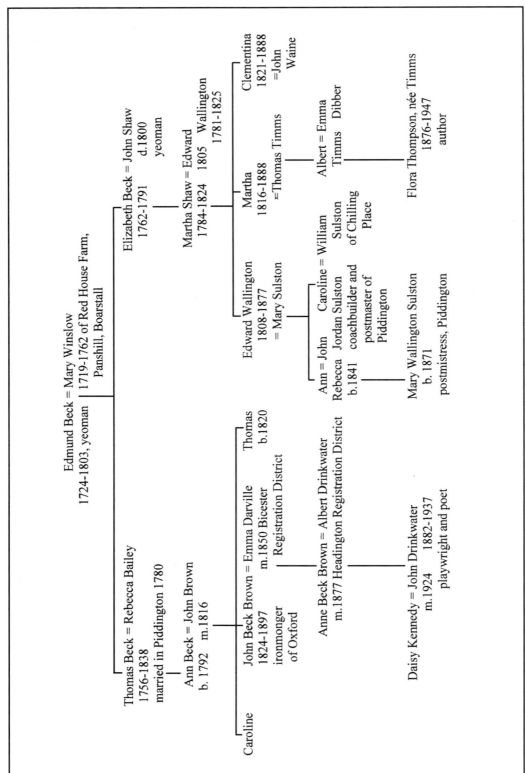

Family tree showing the relationship of the poet and dramatist John Drinkwater to Flora Thompson.

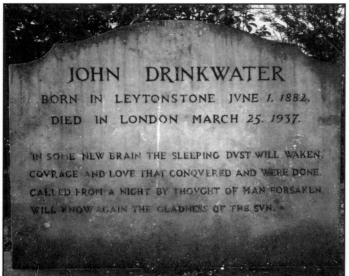

The grave of John Drinkwater (1882-1937) situated in a quiet secluded corner of Piddington churchyard. John Drinkwater's great-great-grandfather Thomas Beck (1756-1838) was the elder brother of Flora's great-great-grandmother Elizabeth Beck (1762-1791), who married John Shaw at Piddington. John Drinkwater recorded the history of his own Beck ancestry and his boyhood days in Piddington in his autobiographies *Inheritance* and *Discovery*. It is just possible that Flora Thompson read these books and his poems and was inspired to write her own autobiography, which became *Lark Rise to Candleford*.

Blackthorn Toll-House, the subject of John Drinkwater's famous poem, the *Toll-House Gate*, published in *Seeds of Time* in 1921. The poem may have had its origins in the local story of the of the apparition of the 'Ludgershall' highwayman, which was periodically seen to gallop along the A41 by the Gallows near Gallows Bridge, Ludgershall, and Blackthorn Toll-House on cold winter nights. When John Drinkwater walked from Bicester's LMS railway station to his uncle's Manor Farm-house at Piddington for his summer holidays, his journey took him past the Toll-House, which was then home to its last solitary occupant, William Arkell (known locally as Billy), who was found one day drowned in Blackthorn's Weir Pond.

The farmhouse now known as *Brown's Piece* in the centre of Piddington. Flora's grandmother Martha was born here in 1816, along with most of Martha's brothers and sisters between 1806 and 1821. In 1824 and 1825 Martha's parents Edward and Martha Wallington, along with several of their children, died here, probably from cholera contracted from infected water obtained from the farmhouse well. The well may have been contaminated by water draining from the village pond, which was situated immediately north of the house. In the 19th century the pond was commonly used by Piddington farmers to water cows and horses and wash local carts. (Courtesy of Martin Haslett)

A steam-driven lorry made by Fodens of Sandbach, Cheshire, standing in front of *Brown's Piece*, the child-hood home of Flora Thompson's grand-mother Martha Wallington, c1920. The driver was delivering flour to Joseph Humphries' bakery, which was located in the yard across the road. The lorry travelled at an average speed of only five miles an hour.

23.ᵈ Nov.ʳ 1805 On which day personally appeared —
Edward Wallington of Ludgershall in the County of Bucks
Yeoman and upon his oath alledged as follows That he is
a bachelor aged twenty one years and upwards,
and that he intends to marry with Martha Shaw
of Piddington in the County of Oxford Spinster aged
twenty one years and upwards And that he doth
not know or believe that there is any lawful let
or impediment to hinder the said intended —
Marriage And that he hath had his usual —
place of abode for four weeks last past in the
said parish of Ludgershall And therefore he prayed
Licence to solemnize the said intended Marriage
in the parish Church of Ludgershall aforesaid

Sworn the above named
Edward Wallington to the
truth of the Premises —
before me W. Stockins Surr..

Edward Wallington

Marriage licence allegation dated 23 November 1805 for the marriage of Edward Wallington of Ludgershall to Martha Shaw of Piddington, the great grand-parents of Flora Thompson, who married at Ludgershall. (Courtesy of the Centre for Buckinghamshire Studies)

The house in Swinton Street, London, where Flora Thompson's great-aunts Elizabeth and Clementina Wallington lived from c1828 until Elizabeth's death in 1839, working as dressmakers. Elizabeth Wallington made a Prerogative Court of Canterbury will here leaving her property to her sisters Clementina and Martha (Flora's grandmother), who received a writing desk.

John Jordan Sulston (1846-1930) holding a box plane in his right hand in front of the doors to his wheelwright's shop near *Brown's Piece* in c1900. John Drinkwater visited the yard as a boy and includes a description in his autobiography. John Jordan Sulston married Anne Rebecca Wallington, first cousin to Flora Thompson's father Albert Timms. Apart from operating the wheelwright's shop from 1870 to 1928, John and Anne ran the Post-Office situated in the adjacent thatched cottage. John Jordan Sulston acted as the sub-postmaster. The Piddington Post Office was eventually taken over by his daughter Mary Wallington Reynolds.

The Sulston family of Lower Farm, Cow Leys, Piddington, c1910. The two elderly members of the family seated in the centre are believed to be William Sulston and his wife. The lady on the far right is Eva Chester, who married William's son John Andrew Sulston in 1910.

Band members leading the procession of Piddington Friendly Society into Mr Chester's bakery yard in Piddington c1910. One member carries a staff of office and another wearing a panama-style hat carries a flag bearing the words *Piddington Friendly Society established 1862*. John Jordan Sulston's wheelwright's yard can be seen in the background opposite.

Baker William Chester (1839-1916) with his baker's cart in his yard directly opposite *Brown's Piece*, c1900. He made deliveries with his cart as far afield as Launton. His daughter Maud married Joseph Humphries, baker and his daughter Eva, married John Andrew Sulston, farmer of Cow Leys, Piddington.

AMBROSDEN and BLACKTHORN

According to local folklore Ambrosden has connections with the Devil. In 1823 John Dunkin recorded a tradition in *The History and Antiquities of the Hundreds of Bullingdon and Ploughley* that: *'their parish church was originally intended to have been erected in a field (then) known by the name of Church Lays; and that the workmen actually proceeded to lay the foundation, but to their astonishment, found that the whole of their materials were moved to Ambrosden during the night. Despairing therefore, of overcoming the activity of their supernatural opponent, the parishioners acquiesced in his choice of a situation, and the building proceeded without further interruption.'*

Church Leys field was actually in Blackthorn, a hamlet in Ambrosden parish. This story about the church being moved by the Devil is found in several Oxfordshire villages and elsewhere and may originate in an attempt to explain place names. Another local custom was that a flagon of ale and a cake were brought by the vicar to Ambrosden church porch after a funeral, possibly a relic of the practice of sin eating, when a man was paid to eat and drink after a funeral to take upon himself the sins of the dead man.

It has been suggested that Ambrosden got its name from Ambrosius Aurelius, who is said to have camped here when Alchester was besieged by the Anglo-Saxons, but a more prosaic explanation, suggested by medieval forms such as *Ambresdone*, is that it means *Ambre's Hill*. Ambrosden was a 'closed' village, under the tight control of the lord of the manor, whereas Blackthorn was an 'open' village where anyone could settle. The villagers enjoyed pasture rights in Bernwood Forest, paying the keeper at Boarstall 24 hens at Christmas, 24 bushels of oats at Easter and 480 eggs and performing services in payment for the rights.

The church of St Mary has a 12th century Romanesque arch and more building work took place throughout the Middle Ages, mostly under the supervision of the canons of Ashridge, who owned the advowson, while Ursula Denton restored the chancel in the 17th century. In the 13th century Ambrosden was one of the richest Oxfordshire churches.

When Sir William Glynne purchased the manor in 1673, he may have moved into the medieval manor house built by Ashridge College on the site of the present Park Farm, which was taxed in 1665 as having thirteen hearths. However, Sir William built a new manor house behind the church. He served as Member of Parliament for Woodstock and is notable for having presented White Kennett (1660-1728), the prominent antiquary who became Bishop of Peterborough, as vicar of Ambrosden in 1685. Kennett published *Parochial Antiquities Attempted in the History of Ambrosden, Burcester and other adjacent parts in the counties of Oxford and Bucks* in 1695, dedicated to Sir William.

The next owner was Sir Edward Turner (1691-1735), a wealthy merchant and member of Lincolns Inn, who married Mary, daughter of Sir Gregory Page, an immensely wealthy director of the East India Company. He too became a director and later chairman of the company. Both men made a great deal of money selling South Sea stock before the bubble burst. He was created a baronet in 1733. His son Edward (1719-1766), who was a distinguished scholar at Balliol College, married Cassandra Leigh, niece of the Master. He too was a member of Lincolns Inn and served as Member of Parliament for Great Bedwin in Wiltshire, the county of Oxfordshire and Penrhyn in Cornwall. His daughter Elizabeth married Colonel Twistleton, who became Lord Saye and Sele of Broughton.

Edward decided to replace Sir William's mansion in 1740, although it was only about seventy years old. He paid £4000 for the house, designed by his close friend, the notable architect Sanderson Miller, reusing stone from the former house and adding new stone from Stone Pits quarry at Blackthorn, and Bibury stone for facing. The façade was 200 feet long, with eleven pedimented windows and a rusticated basement. It was approached along a semi-circular tree-lined avenue. He also had the extensive parkland, five miles in circumference, landscaped with lakes and clumps of trees and statues. Turner's strong relationship with Miller featured in a political pamphlet entitled *The Canvassing Couple or a Trip to the House of Commons, with scenes, machines and other decorations. Particularly a new scene in the Gothick Taste designed by Mr M-ll-r.*

His son Sir Gregory Page Turner (1748-1805) considered the house to be too large and, on failing to pull down part of it to make it smaller, had the complete building demolished, and no further manor houses were built in Ambrosden. Sir Gregory was Sheriff of Oxfordshire in 1783.

Local entertainment included horse racing held in Ambrosden Old Park, although this was the subject of scandal: the *Oxford Journal* commented in 1829 that it was attended by a thousand idlers characterised by 'dullness and stupidity' and that there were several episodes of brutal fighting. However, the main occupation among the villagers up to the Second World War was agriculture, particularly dairy farming, augmented by stone quarrying and brickmaking. Population reached a peak in 1851 when there were 172 inhabitants in Ambrosden and 417 in Blackthorn, then declined until the Central Ordnance Depot was established in 1941. A large housing development for military personnel followed in the 1950s, although the depot is now smaller and some of the houses have been sold for civilian use.

Rowland Herring, author of *I Remember Blackthorn*, published in 1998, wrote that his father was a baker, and other tradesmen included the blacksmith, the butcher, the village shop, a cobbler, a carpenter and a village handyman. Pedlars came to the village: Hedges and Evans with fabrics and drapery, Mr Cherry with ironmongery, Mr Knibbs with fish, Mr Miles with paraffin and Billy Green, who sold the *Christian Herald* and oddments. Sometimes gypsies visited, selling clothes pegs and charms and offering to tell fortunes. Recreation was provided by the *Rose and Crown* and the *Royal Oak*.

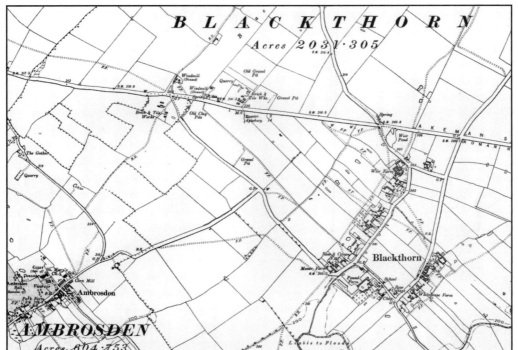

Ordnance Survey map showing the village of Ambrosden and the neighbouring hamlet of Blackthorn in 1900.

Earthen rampart banks found on the south-eastern slopes of Graven Hill during tree felling in the mid 1960s. The ramparts were sectioned in the late 1990s by Professor Eberhard Sauer, but failed to provide an accurate building date. It is possible that they were constructed in the 9th century by Ethelred (died in 871) and his brother Alfred (849-899), who are documented as having fought an unsuccessful battle against the Danes near Graven Hill.

The main street of Ambrosden looking south-west in 1907. The wheelwright's shop on the left behind the railings is believed to have been the premises of carpenter and wheelwright George Eldridge. Further along the street a brewery dray can be seen delivering beer to the *Turner's Arms*.

The main street of Ambrosden looking in the opposite direction in 1904.

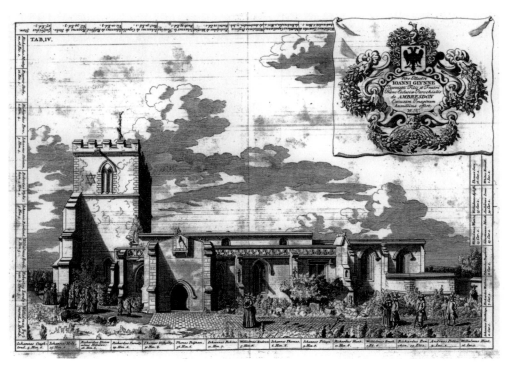

Prospect of Ambrosden Church drawn for White Kennett in 1695. Parts of the church are Norman, although much was rebuilt in the 14th century. On the north side a 12th century doorway survives with roll-mouldings and cushion capitals. Flora Thompson's grandparents Martha Wallington and Thomas Timms were married here in 1844, and Martha's sister Clementina married John Waine here in 1841. Clementina and John Waine had the tenancy of a small farm in Arncott and it is possible that Martha and Thomas Timms stayed with them for a while before moving to St Albans.

Copy of the marriage certificate of Flora Thompson's grandparents Thomas and Martha Timms, who were married by licence at Ambrosden on 18 November 1844. The officiating minister was the Revd J. Cleobury, who took part in the Wallington Chancery court case in London in 1829 and 1830 and had been a friend of Martha Timms for some years.

Portrait of the Revd White Kennett (1660-1728) by James Fittler, ARA. White Kennett served variously as Curate of Bicester, Vicar of Ambrosden, and finally as Bishop of Peterborough. He wrote the celebrated *History and Antiquities of Ambrosden and Burcester*, which was printed at the Sheldonian Theatre Press, Oxford, in 1695. Early in his life he was injured in a serious shooting accident at Middleton Stoney, after which he was obliged to wear a velvet black patch on his forehead to cover the scar. The patch can be seen in the portrait extending just below the front of his wig.

The Bayfield sisters were the daughters of the Revd Charles Bayfield, Vicar of Ambrosden. Typical of the daughters of the clergy in the early 1900s, they involved themselves in charitable works, including raising funds for the Bicester section of the Red Cross and Bicester's Hospital for wounded soldiers. In the photograph the Miss Bayfields are seen in a gig outside the Malthouse in Victoria Road, Bicester, after visiting the Mountain family at 16 and 18 Sheep Street.

Ambrosden church and vicarage viewed from the walled park in front of the former Ambrosden House, c1910. The site of the demolished house is now covered by housing development but in the 1930s the ruined walls of underground cellars remained and were a favourite playground of local children who knew them as the catacombs.

A view of Ambrosden House, the seat of Chief Justice Sir William Glynne, drawn for White Kennett in 1695. Sir William bought the cloister buildings of the former Bicester Priory in c1670 and completely demolished them to provide building stone for the construction of his house at Ambrosden, which survived until 1740 when it was demolished to make way for Sir Edward Turner's 'new' Ambrosden House.

Sir Edward Turner's 'new' Ambrosden House as it appeared two years before it was demolished by his son Sir Gregory Page Turner in 1768. The house and the follies in the grounds were the work of architect Sanderson Miller. For a period of just twenty-eight years the house was the home of Sir Edward Turner and his wife Cassandra, née Leigh, who was the second cousin of the writer Jane Austen.

The memorial to Sir Edward and Lady Cassandra Turner in the vestry of St Edburg's parish church, Bicester. Sir Edward Turner (1719-1766) took part and lost heavily financially in the 1754 Oxfordshire election, which was contested by Philip, Viscount Wenman, Sir James Dashwood and Thomas, Viscount Parker. John Shaw, Flora Thompson's great-great-grandfather, had business dealings with Sir Edward and Lady Turner and was their tenant. Following Sir Edward's death a locked bureau was found in his study at Ambrosden which contained over 50,000 gold guinea pieces. Sir Edward died in 1766 and Lady Cassandra died in 1770, both aged 48. The memorial states that Sir Edward served in three parliaments and *'he exerted himself as an active and vigilant magistrate; adopted early in life the noblest political Principles and he Persevered in them to the end. He was learned without vanity, Religious without Ostentation, and excelled in the great Characters of Husband, Father and Friend.'* Lady Cassandra was described as *'beautiful in Person and engaging in her Manners, won the esteem of all who knew her. A shining Example of Conjugal Affection, and every Christian virtue. To her Children an indulgent Mother, to Servants a kind Mistress, to the Poor living and dying a compassionate Benefactress.'* (Illustrated in John Dunkin's, *History and Antiquities of the Hundreds of Bullingdon and Ploughley*, Vol.1, 1823).

Roman occupation at Blackthorn is known from widespread local finds of pottery and coins. While it is possible there may have been a villa, it is more likely that a Romano-Celtic temple stood on the south-facing slopes of Blackthorn Hill where the road crosses the Chiltern railway line between Blackthorn crossroads and Launton village. Field-work here has produced a pre-conquest intaglio from a ring of Augustan age and many Roman coins which may

have been deposited as votive offerings. The accompanying photograph shows one of a series of four Romano-Celtic temples excavated at Frilford, near Oxford, in July 2007. A similar temple may have stood on the top of Blackthorn Hill. The Frilford temple seen here is typical of its type and had a central cella (which originally contained a shrine) surrounded by a portico.

The site of Blackthorn Village green in front of Kiln and Fir Tree farms, looking south-east towards the former school, congregational church and Pound farmhouse. White Kennett records in his *Parochial Antiquities*:'*that there was seldom any public wedding at Blackthorn that was not accompanied by the custom of riding at the Quintain on the village green.*'

Kennett suggested that the custom of *'Riding at the Quintain'* was of Roman origin and

recorded in the 17th century that the practice still took place at Blackthorn and Deddington. It is just possible that the survival of the custom at Blackthorn had its roots in the Roman military training operations which are known to have taken place on the military practice ground recently discovered at Alchester, some two miles away.

The floods of June 1903, adjacent to the cottages of Shaw's Yard. The signpost of one of Blackthorn's two public houses, *The Royal Oak*, is visible in the distance.

Shaw's Yard, Blackthorn, named after the Shaw family of butchers and carriers who lived here from 1812 to 1968. In 1871 twelve members of the Shaw family were resident: George Shaw, butcher, aged 51, his wife Sarah, née Wilkins, aged 51, and their children, Ann, aged 19, James, aged 17, Ellen, aged 15, George, aged 14, John, aged 3, and Henry, aged 2 (grandson); and next door were George Shaw's brother John, aged 57, carrier, his wife Sarah, aged 53, Ellen, aged 26 (daughter), and granddaughter Sarah, aged 9.

James Shaw, butcher, baker and carrier of Shaw's Yard (1787-1862). He was head of the Shaw family and purchased and moved into Shaw's Yard, Station Road, with his wife Anne, née Hitchcock, in 1812. James was born at Idbury on the Oxfordshire/Gloucestershire border and married Ann (descended from a line of Hitchcock farmers from Launton and Twyford) by licence at Piddington in 1810. Although by trade a butcher and baker, James operated a carriers service with his son John from Blackthorn to the *King's Head*, Bicester. James was buried at Ambrosden, where there is a gravestone to his memory. John Dunkin records in his *History of the Bullingdon and Ploughley Hundreds* that in 1814 James Shaw allowed his bakehouse to be used as an independent meeting house which caused great consternation amongst Bicester's High Anglican circle.

George Shaw (1820-1895), butcher of Shaw's Yard, Blackthorn, the son of James and Ann Shaw. George Shaw was the best man at the wedding of Flora Thompson's grandparents at Ambrosden in 1844 and was presumably a close family friend. The photograph shows him in old age in the early 1890s wearing leather-buttoned breeches, jacket and a top hat.

Sarah Shaw, née Wilkins, who was baptised at Ambrosden on 21 February 1819 and married George Shaw of Blackthorn at Islington Parish Church on 20 March 1851. Sarah's father was John Wilkins, carpenter, who was a paid-up member of the Greyhound Friendly Society at Marsh Gibbon. He died in the cholera epidemic at Blackthorn Hill in 1831 and surviving records of the Greyhound Club show that members contributed £2 towards the cost of his funeral.

Henry Shaw (1868-1918) in his Queen's Own Oxfordshire Hussars uniform at the time of the Boer War. Henry was born at Shaw's Yard and died on active service in 1918. His name appears on the tablet of war dead which formerly hung on the wall of Blackthorn Independent Chapel. He married Clara Ward, a teacher, at Ambrosden in 1893 and they had three children, the youngest of whom Robert, or Bob as he was locally known, died at Shaw's Yard in 1968. Bob Shaw (a butcher) was the last of the Shaw family to live at Shaw's Yard.

The Royal Oak, Blackthorn, before it closed as a public house.

The signboard of the *Royal Oak* showing Charles II in the Boscobel Oak. It records the episode when the king hid from Parliamentary soldiers in the canopy of a large oak tree at Boscobel after his defeat at the Battle of Worcester in 1651.

The floods in front of Fir Tree farm and neighbouring cottages at Blackthorn in 1906. Flooding in Blackthorn village was an annual problem in the early 1900s when it was common practice for local families to live upstairs during the two or three weeks of heavy flooding during the early summer months. The low thatched building in the centre of the photograph is a pig sty. A rear extension to Fir Tree farmhouse incorporates stonework brought from the demolition of Ambrosden House in the late 18th century.

James Jones (1829-1906), farmer of Kiln and Pound Farms in Blackthorn, who married Martha Waine at Ambrosden parish church in April 1853. James was the head of the Jones family who were important farmers in Blackthorn and Marsh Gibbon throughout the 19th and 20th centuries.

Martha Jones (1829-1877), née Waine, wife of James Jones, farmer, of Blackthorn. Martha was born at Witney, the daughter of Thomas Waine (1787-1871), farmer, and his wife Rachel, née Fox, and died at Blackthorn giving birth to her thirteenth child in 1877. She was the younger sister of John Waine, who married Flora Thompson's great-aunt Clementina Wallington at Ambrosden in 1841.

Martha Jones, née Waine, and her husband James Jones and their family at Kiln Farm, Blackthorn, in 1862. Their eldest child, Esther Anne, born in 1854, stands in the centre. Charles Waine Jones, born 1861, sits on his father's knee. (Courtesy of David Markham)

The Jones family at Kiln Farm in c1900. Back row, left to right: Herbert, Joseph, James, David and Charles Waine Jones. Middle row, left to right: Martha, Louisa, James Jones, senior (born 1829), Esther and Betsy Waine Jones. Front row, seated: Rose, Eva and Polly Jones.

The Independent Chapel, Blackthorn, in c1900. For many years this photograph hung on the walls of the Joneses' farmhouses at Kiln and New House Farms, Blackthorn. The cost of building the church and the neighbouring school was £390. James Jones of Kiln and Pound Farms is reported to have donated £100, placing it on the chapel's foundation stone at the laying in 1869 and telling assembled onlookers 'to get on with the good work.' The church was officially registered in June 1870 by Jonas Paxton, Superintendent Registrar for the Bicester District, for the solemnisation of marriages.

The rear of New House farmhouse shortly after Charles Waine Jones and his family moved there. He acquired it with a loan from Tubb's Bank in Bicester in 1902, which generated the following letter sent to Charles's father, James.

Tubbs Bank, Bicester
November 22nd 1902.

Mr James Jones

Dear Sir,

Mr. James Jones promised me the additional security and I shall expect him to give it to me. If he had not promised I should never have lent his son the money to send to the Ecclesiastical Commissioners for deposit on New House Farm. You must keep him up to the mark.

Yours faithfully,
Henry Tubb

Charles Waine Jones's son Tom with a cart-horse outside the back of Kiln Farm, Blackthorn in 1912.

Elfreda, Vera and Agnes Jones with two pet lambs they had adopted, at New House farm in 1910. Many local farming families allowed their children to keep orphaned lambs as pets around the house and reared them on bottled milk. A Bicester family living in Sheep Street kept a pet lamb called Jill which used to walk around the town with the family dog for the first year of its life. When the lamb grew too large, it was returned to the farm.

Combining at New House farm in the 1930s. The man on the combine is probably Tom Jones.

Hay-carting with an Oxfordshire wagon at New House farm in August 1930.

The same Oxfordshire wagon seen in the previous photograph, painted in the characteristic Oxfordshire colours of red for the wheels and yellow for the body, which was made for Charles Waine Jones of New House Farm, Blackthorn, in 1918. When they sold New House Farm in 1970, Mr Jones's daughters Evelyn and Elfreda donated the wagon to the Oxfordshire Museum service and it is now on show at Cogges Manor Farm Museum, Witney, which was tenanted in the 19th century by the Hollis family, who were cousins of the Jones family (Martha Hollis, née Waine, was the aunt of Martha Waine, wife of James Jones).

Wheat-thrashing with a horse-drawn thrashing machine at New House farm, Blackthorn, in 1910. The men next to the machine on the right are building a rick with the thrashed stalks. The man on the far right is Blackthorn baker, John Herring.

Members of the Green and Shaw families photographed in front of Brickyard Cottage, Blackthorn Hill, after the marriage of Jane Green to Frederick Adcock at Ambrosden parish church
on 3 August 1886. Jane, the daughter of William Green, brickmaker, of Blackthorn Hill (1830-
1906) and his wife Alice, née Langford, was born in 1864 at the brickyard located near the
Heathfield Cross roads at Bletchingdon. The groom, Frederick, came from Buckingham and
until 1913 operated as a successful clothier at 13 Market Square, twice acting as mayor of
Buckingham. Family members in the photograph are - back row, left to right: Amos Green,
brickmaker, ? , Richard Adcock, Mrs Adcock (aunt to groom), Mr Adcock (uncle to groom),
Maria King, James Shaw, licensee of the King's Head, Finmere, and his wife Emily, née
Green. Middle row, left to right: Sarah Shaw, née Wilkins (1819-1896), of Shaw's Yard, Blackthorn, William Green (1830-1906), brickmaker, Frederick Adcock, Jane Adcock, née Green,
and Alice Green (1834-1922) - known locally as 'Granny Green'. Front row, left to right: Emma
Green, née Timberlake, James Green, brickmaker and tile manufacturer, Amos Green, junior,
George Green, brickmaker, Ellen Green, Ann Shaw, and ?. The Green family rented the Blackthorn brickyard from the Page Turner estate and had a kiln at Blackthorn Hill and another
at Horton-cum-Studley. According to the late Mrs Bertha Green of Tower Farm, Boarstall,
members of the family including herself took it in turns to sit around the coal-fired kilns during firings, which lasted three days. The matriarch of the Green family was William Green's
wife Alice, who lived at Blackthorn Hill until she died aged eighty-seven. She smoked a clay
pipe and took a pinch of snuff daily.

Brickyard Cottage, the original home of brickmakers William and Alice Green at Blackthorn Hill. Between 1880 and 1927, the Greens operated a brickworks in the field beyond the 18th century windmill, which included a brick kiln, a lime kiln and a rectangular claypit served by a narrow gauge railway. The photograph was taken by Stanley Freese in the 1930s. (Courtesy of James Venn)

Alice Green, née Langford (1834-1922), wife of William Green, brickmaker of Blackthorn Hill, photographed at the brickyard shortly before she died. Alice wears a sun bonnet to protect her head from the sun.

BLACKTHORN BRICK YARD,
NEAR BICESTER.

58,250 BUILDING BRICKS
1,924 PAVING BRICKS, 948 COPING BRICKS,

81,513 DRAINING PIPES,
(Sizes from Two to Nine inches),

14,128 PLAIN HOUSE TILES,
345 Ridge Tiles, 240 Gutter Tiles, 210 Hip Tiles, 1,142 Pan Tiles, 1,160 Garden Edge Tiles, 124 9-inch Flooring Squares, 26 yards of Pitching Stones, 90 Planking Stones, Quantity of Fine Gravel, Lime Stones, Sundry odd Bricks, Stones and Sawdust; also a capital

PIPE, BRICK & TILE MACHINE,
With Dies, Racks, &c., complete by "Clayton,"

Water Trough, Pallett Boards, Brick and Tile Moulds, 6 Brick Barrows, 5 Box Barrows, 4 Bearing-off Barrows, 2 Tables, Stools, Trestles, 3 Iron Stone-drills, 3 Kiln Rakes, 3 Stone-digging Bars, 4 Sledge Hammers, 12 Deal Planks, 4 Battens, Ladder and Tools, &c.,
THE PROPERTY OF MR. JAMES JONES, WHO IS LEAVING THE BRICK YARD.
WILL BE SOLD BY AUCTION, BY MESSRS.

JONAS PAXTON, SON, & HOLIDAY

ON THE PREMISES,
On Thursday, November 19th, 1885, at 12 o'clock,

The above will be sold in convenient lots to suit all purchasers
Catalogues may be had at the Inns in the Neighbourhood; or of the Auctioneers, Bicester, Banbury and Deddington.

SMITH AND PANKHURST, PRINTERS, BICESTER.

Notice for the sale of the contents of the Blackthorn Brickyard on 19 November 1885, which was then the property of James Jones of Kiln Farm, Blackthorn.

James Green making bricks in a wooden mould in the late 1880s. To the right stands his wife Emma, née Timberlake, with her eldest son in a pram.

The family of James Green (1856-1927), brickmaker, of Blackthorn Hill and Horton-cum-Studley in 1910. James was the eldest son of William Green of Blackthorn Hill. Back row, left to right: William Green, known as Will (1894-1976), farmer, of Pans Hill farm and Tower farm, Boarstall, Alice Cashmore and Harry Green. Sitting, left to right: Emma Green, née Timberlake (sister of George Timberlake, manager of the Eclipse Mineral Water Factory, Bicester), and her husband James Green. Sitting on the floor in front is Thomas George Green, who was killed in the First World War on 19 April 1917, aged 21. He served in the Oxon and Bucks Light Infantry and his name is listed on the Thiepval memorial in France. The Green family originated from North Leigh where the family can be traced back to the 18th century.

The Greens' brick kiln in a field at Horton-cum-Studley.

ALCHESTER

Alchester was the legionary fortress of the Second Augusta Legion and one of two Roman towns in Oxfordshire. The extensive site remains relatively undisturbed in farmland one mile south of Bicester on the edge of Wendlebury parish. In the 17th and 18th centuries its fame gave rise to a local rhyme:

> *In Oxfordshire, by Graven-Hill Wood,*
> *Stood Alchester so fair and good;*
> *Allectus' walls are brought full low,*
> *Where once they stood now corn doth grow,*

According to legend Alchester played a part in the political struggles between the usurping British emperor Carausius and his minister Allectus. In his *History of Ardley, Bucknell, Caversfield and Stoke Lyne* (1894), Launton historian, the Revd James Blomfield ventured that Allectus had killed Carausius in battle at Carausius Field (Caversfield), north of Bicester, and that he and other Roman dead were buried under a mound within a square enclosure near Caversfield churchyard.

The antiquary William Stukeley (1687-1765), who explored the site, probably rightly considered Alchester to be the Roman Alauna of the *Ravenna Cosmography*. Stukeley wrote:

The city was fenced with a bank and ditch all around. It is a square of 1000 feet, each side standing on the four cardinal points; these sides are easily discernable at the corners, at each of which the country people say stood a tower to defend it; and that the brook also originally ran around it. On the west of the city, a little distance from the city ditch is an artificial hill, called Castle Hill, full of Roman bricks, stones and foundations.

John Dunkin recorded in his *History of Bicester and Alchester* that Stukeley's 'castle' mound was opened in 1766 by the proprietor Mr Penrose, who found the remains of a tumbled walled enclosure containing a centrally placed building still standing four feet high, with a hypocaust and a coloured mosaic pavement. Dunkin visited Alchester in 1814 and saw many fragments of red, green and blue Roman pottery and many coins, which the locals called Alchester pennies.

Scientific excavations in the 1920s and 1930s directed by Professors Christopher Hawkes and John Iliffe confirmed that the archaeological stratigraphy was preserved to a depth of several feet and that twenty-five acres of the overall settlement extending over one hundred acres had been walled, gated and ditched. Christopher Young's 1974 excavations revealed that the eight-foot-wide town wall was backed by a contemporary earthen rampart and fronted by a defensive ditch. Excavations at the west gate in 2002 to 2003 suggested that the wall and rampart were constructed in the late 2nd or 3rd century.

The remarkable discovery of twenty-three fragments of a tombstone belonging to Lucius Valerius Geminus from North Italy, a legionary of the Second Augusta Legion, were found in the footings of the town wall. He died in about A.D. 60 aged 50 years, and must have received a grant of land at Alchester from the Roman authorities on his retirement after twenty-five years' military service. The tombstone is one of the most important Roman discoveries ever made in central England.

A programme of aerial photography, resistivity surveys and eight years of summer excavations (concluding in 2003) have concentrated west of the walled Roman town in the field containing Stukeley's 'castle'. Here a military annexe was found next to the legionary fortress for the Second Augusta Legion. Stumps of three massive timber posts from a tower flanking the west gate of the annexe provided a dendrochronology date of A.D. 44 for the felling of the timbers. Eberhard Sauer, the director, has argued that much of the fortress lies under the walled Roman town and that he has found the remains of a double granary and part of the ditch system of the fortress near the south-west angle of the town wall. Sauer postulates that the fortress was the main base for the Second Augusta Legion from A.D. 43 until the A.D. 50s. Alchester may also have served for a time as the headquarters of Claudius's invasion force commander Aulus Plautius and it is possible that the Alchester legionary garrison itself was commanded by the future Emperor Vespasian.

Alchester developed from a *vicus* settlement, which grew up to the north, east and west of the legionary fortress in the middle of the first century. The town became the most important Roman nucleated settlement in Oxfordshire and may have been the administrative centre for the Upper Thames Valley.

Work in 1892 revealed the remains of a small gravelled forum with a portico on three sides, backed by a large rectangular building, which has been interpreted as a temple or council chamber. The courtyard measured some 40 metres across. A fragment of an inscription found near the town's north gate in 1991 may be a dedicatory inscription to the Emperor and possibly from this building. A Flavian date (A.D. 68-96) for this structure seems a strong possibility.

Aerial photographs taken by Major Allen and Professor J. K. St Joseph clearly show the outline of the porticoed forum and associated temple or council chamber plus a concentration of narrow-fronted shops, workshops and strip houses along the two major stone-paved streets which bisect the defended area. Away from the shops, courtyard houses and several small temples have been identified in the more open areas adjacent to the rear of the town walls. To the west of the defended area, Stukeley's 'castle' can now be identified as a public baths within a rectangular walled precinct which may have originated as a first-century legionary bath-house. Two small classical temples have been identified situated immediately east of the baths.

George James Dew (1846-1928), a local relieving officer and amateur antiquary, bought Roman coins from Wendlebury agricultural labourers working on the site of Alchester in the 1880s and 1890s. The dates of these suggest that the town was occupied continuously from the Neronian period (A.D. 54-68) to c. A.D. 410. Very worn late 4th and early 5th century coins suggest that the town may have continued to operate as a market to the mid 5th century. Dunkin proposed that the town was later completely abandoned and that Birinus, Bishop of Dorchester, took building material from it for his new minster church and town at Bicester. The end of the town as a viable settlement may have been caused by the rising water-table which forced the Romans to raise ground levels within the walled area by two to three feet.

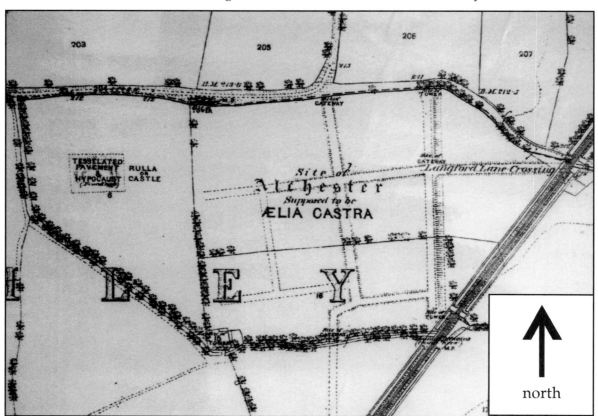

Ordnance Survey map showing the site of the twenty-five acre walled town of Alchester published in 1881. The site of the public baths marked 'tesselated pavement and hypocaust' in the field beyond the site of the west gate can be plainly seen.

An engraving from the second edition of William Stukeley's *Itinerarium Curiosum* published in 1773, which represents one of the earliest pictorial representations of the Roman town and shows the Roman road from Silchester to Towcester running through the site of the defended area. The town of Bicester and the tower of St Edburg's parish church are visible on the horizon one mile to the north.

Another engraving of Alchester, drawn by J. and H.S. Storer for John Dunkin's *History and Antiquities of the Ploughley and Bullingdon Hundreds* (1823), showing William Stukeley's 'castle' in the foreground (now identified as the site of the public baths) and in the background, Graven Hill. Graven Hill may have been the site of a Roman signal station which forwarded messages to Alchester and other signal stations along Akeman Street. Clearance of woodland on the south-eastern slopes of Graven Hill in the 1960s revealed the earthen ramparts of what appears to have been a small Dark-Age fort, which may have been connected with the local military activities of Kings Alfred and Ethelred.

The remains of two massive timber posts belonging to a tower flanking the west gate of the military annexe to the legionary fortress of the Second Augusta Legion at Alchester. The timber gave a dendrochronology date of A.D. 44 for felling and has helped to prove that Alchester had a military presence almost from the beginning of the Roman conquest. It seems likely that the fortress was abandoned militarily by the A.D. 60s to provide soldiers for a more northern frontier.

The pitched-stone foundation of the east wall of the Roman town of Alchester, sectioned by Christopher Young in August 1974, which was fronted by a defensive ditch and backed by an earthen rampart bank constructed in the late 2nd or 3rd century. From excavations conducted between 1998 and 2003 on Alchester's military annexe it would appear that the Roman town wall and rampart overlie large sections of the defences of a legionary fortress of the Second Augusta Legion.

An early 2nd century Poppy Head beaker found at Alchester in 1971; part of an assemblage of broken 2nd century pottery (including a mica-dusted dish, a cooking pot and a Samian bowl) and three coins of the Emperor Marcus Aurelius found immediately adjacent to a human inhumation. The pottery may have belonged in life to the buried person and may have been deliberately broken and buried as a part of a funeral ritual.

Traditional folksong relating to Langford Brook which passes close to the eastern defences of the walled Roman town of Alchester. It bears a close resemblance to the *Eynsham Poaching Song*.

Langford Brook

Three Bicester chaps went out one day,
To Gregory's manor they went their way;
They took three dogs to search for game,
And soon to Gravenhill Wood they came.
Refrain : Laddie, oh. Laddie, oh.
Whack, fol, lol, laddie oh ;

The first it was a bulldog bold,
The next a spaniel six months old,
The third it was a terrier fine,
And it was up to the poaching line.
Refrain :

They had not been there but half an hour
Before the spaniel put up a hare ;
Then up she jumped, and away she ran ;
The very next moment a pheasant sprang.
Refrain :

They hadn't quite beat the wood all
through
Before Long Shouler came in view.
As soon as they saw that humbug look
Away they leathered for Langford Brook.
Refrain :

Now Langford Brook was up to the brim ;
You'd have laughed to see them swim :
Six feet of water, if not more ;
When they got out their dogs came o'er.
Refrain :

The keeper, he was long and strong ;
Good lord ! How he did pull along :
He pulled till he was out of wind ;
The farther he ran, he got behind.
Refrain :

Swim Langford Brook he would not try,
But stopped he did where it was dry ;
If they'd been caught, as sure as day
They'd have had a month, or a pound to
pay.
Refrain :

So then for home they made their tracks,
With a pheasant and a hare slung on
their backs,
And that was the end of that fine day,
Singing laddie oh, laddie oh, whack fol lay.
Laddie oh. Laddie oh
Whack fol lol laddie oh !

Sledging on the western slopes of Graven Hill near Alchester in January 1928. The occupants of the sledges have been identified from left to right as follows: (Sledge 1) Norman Prentice and his daughter Mary, (2) unknown occupants, (3) Kate Clifton, Edith Gosling (later Mrs Grimes) and Reginald Grimes, (4) Tom Stanford, Ron Buckle and Frederick Waine, (5) Albert Buckle, Edward Benjamin, and ?(6), Jim Waine, Tom Harris and Ian MacDonald Goble. While sledging took place on the slopes of Graven Hill in winter, it was traditional for Bicester and Ambrosden people to go 'primrosing' there on Good Friday. Occasionally when Easters were dry and hot, it could be hazardous as Graven Hill was well known for its colonies of adders, which basked in the sun among the primroses.

Bicester's horse-drawn fire engine, manned by members of Bicester Town Council, temporarily halted at the Langford railway crossing near the Alchester side of Graven Hill on 8 November 1923. The fire engine was deliberately driven out from its engine house in the Launton Road, Bicester, to Langford, to demonstrate the right of wheeled traffic to use the crossing. At this time Graven Hill (in the background) was part of the 2500 acre Page Turner's private estate, which was sold off in blocks in 1930.

BICESTER

Bicester plays a significant role in *Lark Rise to Candleford* as several aspects of it are included in Flora's *Candleford Green*, her town of *Candleford* and *Mixlow* in *Still Glides the Stream*. The Bicester area has been inhabited since at least the Bronze Age with two of the largest local concentrations of Bronze Age and Iron Age barrows having been found on Whitelands Farm (near Bicester Village) and along Skimmingdish Lane (near RAF Bicester). Roman villa estates existed at King's End Farm, occupied from the second to fourth centuries, and at Glory Farm. The rising water-table at the low-lying Roman town of Alchester may have forced the sub-Roman population to migrate to higher ground on the Cornbrash outcrop at Bicester. Earthen rampart banks on the south-eastern slopes of Graven Hill overlooking Ambrosden may be the remains of an Iron Age hillfort or a temporary Dark Age earthwork.

Bicester's earliest Anglo-Saxon remains appear to be 7th and 8th century rectangular aisled long houses found east of the Market Square. In the 7th century Bicester became the centre of an ecclesiastical administrative district and a Saxon minster may have been constructed either in the area of the parish church or near the modern Catholic church (where stone foundations and Anglo-Saxon graves have been excavated) using stone robbed from Alchester's town wall.

The Domesday Book of 1086 suggests that Bicester had 200-250 inhabitants. According to Dunkin, the town developed as two separate communities: King's End to the south of the Bure stream, and Market End to the north. The present triangular shape of the Market Square may delineate the boundaries of a ditch system for a defended burh established in the 10th century by Edward the Elder and the discovery of Roman bricks in the vicinity of the Market Square may indicate that 'a burh' grew up around the site of a Roman mausoleum.

Bicester's growth in the 13th and 14th centuries was stimulated by the foundation of a large Augustinian Priory (1182) by Norman lord Gilbert Basset. Excavations and fieldwork uncovered a large complex of buildings extending over ten acres centred in Old Place Yard, behind St Edburg's church, dominated by the Priory church. This was extended in the early 14th century to house the shrine of St Edburg, presented by the King's cousin, Thomas, Earl of Lancaster. The priory was dissolved in 1536 after its assets had been valued at only £176. The Dissolution valuation seems to have been kept deliberately low to enable early closure, and its true rental value may be more accurately reflected in the large sum of £505, which Roger Moore (a Sergeant of the King's household) paid the Duke of Suffolk for part of the former priory land in 1542. The priory was an important centre for hospitality: Henry VIII visited in 1526 and had a meeting here with his lieutenant in Wales, Sir Edward Don, in September 1534. Elizabeth I visited the Moore family here in 1568, en route to Rycote. A payment book belonging to the Queen survives, listing expenses made for refurbishment of the priory's domestic buildings in readiness for her visit, which includes repairs to doors and staircases and the making of partitions and an entry for making a press in which to store the Queen's clothes.

Much of the Bicester area supported the King during the Civil War, with Boarstall forming a centre of operations. Bicester itself was used as a supply base by both Royalists and Parliamentarians and both Charles I and Oliver Cromwell stayed in the town. Cromwell is believed to have stayed in rooms above 12 Market Square. Economic stability returned after the war and trade was profitable enough for eight tradesmen to issue trade tokens between 1657 and the late 1660s, including John Warry, who issued a heart-shaped brass halfpenny with a design of three clay pipes, and Gabriel Burrows, the ironmonger.

In the late 18th century Thomas Mostyn founded the Bicester Hunt, establishing kennels at Stoke Lyne. Later several hunting boxes, including The Garth in Bicester, were built to accommodate large gatherings of hunting guests and their entourage of servants.

The opening of railway stations in 1850 and 1910 encouraged trade by bringing daily contact with distant parts of the country. Bicester became a thriving market town with a population of 3306 in 1881, with many shops and local industries including clock-making, brewing, the manufacture of ginger beer, tanning and brick-making. There were also several blacksmiths who worked for local members of the Bicester Hunt.

Flora Thompson would have visited Bicester often while working at Fringford and may well have known many of her cousins who worked in the town centre, including stonemason Arthur Edward Waine and wheelwright Thomas Edward Wallington Waine, who worked for builder and shopkeeper Joseph Belsey Layton. The latter may have been one of the inspirations for the character of *James Dowland*, the stonemason of *Candleford*, who was described as her father's cousin.

Flora's depiction of *Dr. Henderson*, the *Candleford Green* doctor, was inspired by Dr Cecil M. Hendriks, the much-loved doctor who was born in Jamaica in 1856. He came to Bicester from London in 1885 at the age of 29 and spent the rest of his life there. He was also medical officer and public vaccinator for the Stoke Lyne district, medical officer to the Post Office, assistant medical officer to the schools, and worked at the Hospital of Infectious Diseases. When he died, he was cremated at Golders Green. His obituary in the *Bicester Advertiser* on 24 July 1925 was fulsome in its praise:

. . . One could recount a host of stories of his kindness, which was proverbial. When he could do good, he did without ostentation. A life such as his will be sadly missed, for it may be said of him that he lived and moved and gave his life and talents for others…

He was also notable for not sending bills to those he felt could not afford to pay them, but on his death his executors found his account books and did send out the bills.

Flora would also have visited the Post Office in Bicester. The postmaster, Walter Joseph

French (Flora's *Mr Rushton*), visited the Fringford Post Office regularly and took quite a shine to Flora. He would have liked to have offered her a job in Bicester, but he already had two maiden ladies working there and neither left to get married, so there was no vacancy for Flora. He became postmaster in Bicester around 1872 and lived next door to the Post Office with his wife Sarah and his three sons. He was a Methodist and, according to Flora, thought that his staff adored him, but behind his back they nicknamed him 'Holy Joe'.

Another Bicester institution which Flora ascribes to *Candleford Green* is the free reading room for labouring men funded by the Earl of Jersey, which was the equivalent of the Mechanics Institute that she mentioned.

The earliest known view of Sheep Street, Bicester, drawn and etched by J. and H.S. Storer in 1822 for the *History of the Bullingdon and Ploughley Hundreds*, Vol. 2, by John Dunkin. On the left can be seen the *Crown Inn* (demolished in c1965), which with the *King's Arms* (on Market Hill) was one of the town's two principal coaching inns. Further up the street can be seen a pole carrying the sign of the *Wheatsheaf Inn* and on the immediate right the *Bear Inn*.

The last cattle and sheep market held in Sheep Street, Bicester, in 1910. For reasons of public health and safety the market was moved to a new site in Victoria Road, which eventually closed for the sale of livestock in the 1980s. The Bicester livestock market was one of the largest in Oxfordshire and attracted farmers from surrounding villages and neighbouring counties. In the 1950s and 1960s the auctioneer was often Sam Miller of Midland Marts. The Market was held on Monday mornings and was usually over by 4 p.m. ready for 'washing down'.

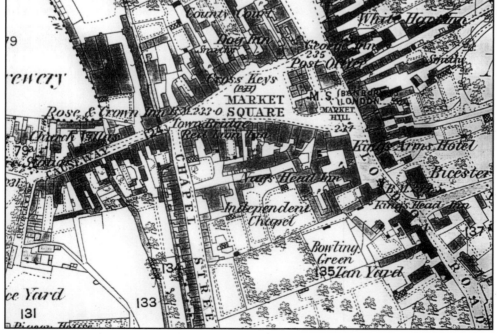

First edition of the 25 inch Ordnance Survey map showing the central part of Bicester in 1881. Clearly marked is the Post Office, then facing the central block of Market Hill, and the well-known Shillingford Brewery in the Causeway, which had an agency for European sales in Paris.

The old Bicester Post Office on the Market Square, very well known to Flora Thompson, is the second building on the right next to the *George Hotel*. Both properties are now gone. The *George* was demolished in 1920 to make way for the Midland Bank and the 'old' Post Office was demolished in the 1970s to make way for a Sketchleys dry-cleaners. Both buildings dated from the 17th century and had extensive cellars. The old Post Office was replaced by a new purpose built one at 56 Sheep Street in 1926, which remained in operation until the 1990s.

Advertisement for the Circulating Library situated at the back of French's stationer's and bookshop at 12 Market Square. Mrs French's husband, Walter Joseph French, acted as postmaster at the Post Office next door from the time of their arrival in Bicester, c1872, until his retirement as postmaster in c1911. After 1911 Mr and Mrs French ran the stationer's shop together until the late 1920s.

The staff of the Bicester Post Office photographed outside the front of the Market Square Post Office in 1915. Back row, left to right: Garbutt, Coles, Clifton, ?, ?, Wilson ?, Jenkins ?, and Spencer ?. Middle row, left to right: Bert Pankhurst (later proprietor of Pankhurst's stationers and the *Bicester Advertiser*), T. Clifton, Dagley, Turney, ?, Hudson?, Hudson, Franklin, Harry Havelock Waine (second cousin of Flora Thompson) and Clifton. Front row, left to right: Dawes, ?, Walter Joseph French (Bicester postmaster c1872 to 1911), ?, ?, ?, and Miss Beatrice Wrapson. When she worked for Mrs Whitton at Fringford, Flora Thompson hoped she might one day transfer to the Post Office at Bicester but was thwarted in doing so by two lady assistants who never moved on. One of these ladies was Miss Beatrice Wrapson of Priory Road (seen at the end of the front row), who worked there for over thirty years. Walter Joseph French, seated in the front row, was the Bicester postmaster on whom Flora based *Mr Rushton*, who visited *Miss Lane* at Candleford Green Post Office for annual inspections. He was born at Buckingham in 1846, the son of Joseph French, a dealer in toys and rags. Walter joined his uncle William Walford, the Buckingham Postmaster and Watchmaker, in Bridge Street and in the 1871 census is described as a telegraph clerk aged 25. He married Sarah Hyde in 1872 and became postmaster at Bicester soon after. He died at Moseley, Birmingham in May 1927 and left an estate at Bicester worth £2677.

Market Hill was an area of Bicester's town centre situated between the island block of the Market Square and the junction with the London Road. This is the view looking north-east in c1900 with Hedges block on the left, demolished 1962/1963, and in the centre the house and shop of builder Joseph Belsey Layton (1849-1901), who may have been an inspiration for Flora Thompson's builder *James Dowland* in *Lark Rise to Candleford.*

Bicester entrepreneur and local builder, Joseph Belsey Layton (1849-1901), photographed with his five-year-old son George (1878-1954) and staff at the back of the Layton shop premises on Market Hill in 1883. Two of Flora Thompson's father's first cousins appear in the photograph: Arthur Edward Waine (1863-1947), stonemason (standing with pole), third from left and Thomas Edward Wallington Waine (1846-1918), wheelwright, of Launton, far right. Other identified members of the Layton staff include carpenter and staircase maker, Joseph Grantham (second from the left) and, seated next to him with watch-chain, foreman Joseph Small.

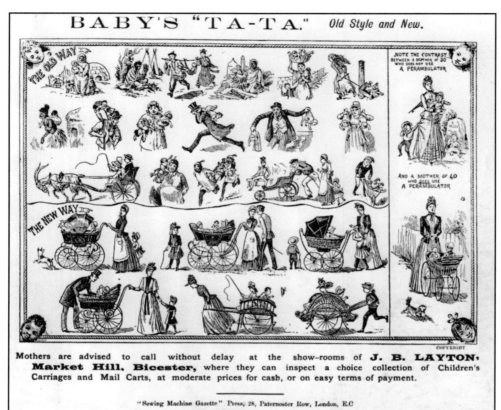

Baby's Ta-Ta, Old Style and New. Advertisement for the sale of children's carriages and mail carts on sale at Joseph Belsey Layton's showroom at Market Hill, Bicester, in 1891.

Tombstone in the Methodist section of Bicester's 'new' cemetery to the memory of Joseph Belsey Layton and his wife Catherine, née Bricknell (who was almost twelve years older than her husband). Joseph and Catherine married in London in 1876.

Postcard showing the London Road approach to Market Hill. Dr Cecil Morgan Hendriks lived at number 5 on the right and was cast by Flora Thompson as *Dr Henderson* in *Lark Rise to Candleford*, and as *'the Old Doctor from Mixlow who never sent out any bills'* in *Still Glides the Stream*. Dr Hendriks's car, one of the first in Bicester, stands in the road outside.

Dr Hendriks stands second from the right, with cap and pointed beard, with wounded soldiers admiring his new motor car outside 5 London Road, Bicester, in 1915. According to local lore, before buying the car, Dr Hendriks visited his village patients in a horse and trap driven by his coachman. In snowy weather he used a sleigh, which glided noiselessly around the country roads. It was the only vehicle of its type in the Bicester area and gave credibility to the story of Father Christmas to the very young.

John Thomas Mountain (1868-1940), the hospital pharmacist, left, seated next to Dr Cecil Morgan Hendriks, right, with the staff of the Bicester Red Cross Hospital in 1917. Mr Mountain's daughter Dorothy, sits in front of her father.

The cement-rendered façade of Robert Burgess Sandiland's chemist shop at 16 and 18 Sheep Street. The shop had been a chemist's since the 1850s and was eventually taken over by Caversham chemist John Thomas Mountain in 1902. The business continued until c1969, when it was sold by Dorothy Adeline Mountain to Mr Bell of Hitchin and closed soon after. John Mountain was also the town optician and photographer. He took many of the images used for postcards sold by Walter Joseph French, the Bicester stationer and postmaster.

Watch and clockmaker Edwin Dealey waiting for a prescription in Mountain's chemist shop in the 1920s. To his right can be seen John Mountain's framed photograph of Bicester Wool fair, which he took in c1903. Also visible is a fine array of glass-stoppered medicine bottles, many of them dating to the time of Robert Burgess Sandiland, who operated as the chemist on the premises between 1851 and 1901.

Chemist John Thomas Mountain was a stalwart member of the Bicester Rifle Club. Here he is seen with William Harris Morgan (1889-1974) in 1920, after they had jointly won the British .22 Rifle shooting competition. Both are wearing specially made shooting jackets. John Mountain operated as a chemist at 16 and 18 Sheep Street from 1902 until his death in 1940, while William Harris Morgan was a professional photographer with a shop on the Market Square. William Harris Morgan was the grandson of Thomas Harris (1808-1875), licensee of the *Fox* at Juniper, and his father was Joseph Morgan, a tailor, who ran Hethe Post Office.

William Grimsley's fishmonger's and game dealer's shop at 5 Sheep Street photographed by William Harris Morgan in 1920. William Grimsley ran his business there from c1875 to the 1920s, and was one of the town's chief fish and game dealers. In the early 1900s his main rival for the sale of game was Aaron Parsons, who operated a shop in the London Road. (Courtesy of Michael Morgan)

A 203 pound halibut resting on a bed of green reeds in front of Grimsley's fish shop in c1910. The shop was just round the corner from the Bicester Post Office and may have inspired Flora Thompson's description of the fishmonger's in *Candleford*, *'where a whole salmon reposed on a bed of green reeds with ice sprinked over. Ice in August! They would never believe it at home.'* (*Lark Rise to Candleford*, p 340).

Opposite Grimsleys, the front of Palmers' ironmonger's shop at 6 and 8 Sheep Street in c1905. Displayed on the pavement and road outside are a range of gardening forks and shovels, a lawn roller, two ploughs and a harrow. Two signs advertise the sale of Carless Petrol for the use of the passing motorist. The shop premises has a date-stone of 1688 and may have operated as an ironmonger's continuously back to the middle of the 17th century. Gabriel Burrows, the well-known Bicester ironmonger in the 1650s and 1660s, may have operated here. He issued his own trade-token and appears to have been a member of the Burrows ironmongery family, which had shops in Thame and Oxford. Flora Thompson's great-great-great-great-grandmother, Frances Burrows (1695-1778), wife of John Shaw of Piddington, was descended from the Oxford branch of the ironmongery family.

The frontage of Gobles', the greengrocer's and fruiterer's at 2 Sheep Street in 1920 photographed by William Harris Morgan. The business also operated as a florist and market garden and was founded by parish constable, James Goble, who came from Sussex. He acquired the property in 1834. The business was carried on by five generations of the family and, like Grimsley the fishmonger, was very close to Bicester Post Office and would have been known to Flora Thompson. His grandson William Wain Goble (1837-1912) was the nephew of John Waine, who married Flora Thompson's great-aunt Clementina Wallington of Piddington. (Courtesy of Michael Morgan).

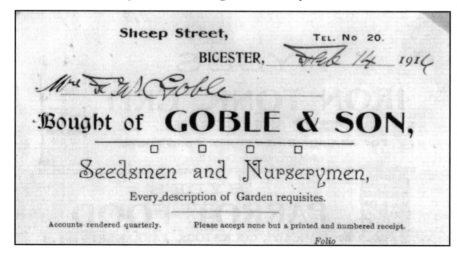

A Goble billhead.

William Wain Goble (1837-1912), greengrocer and florist, photographed with his wife and twelve children behind the family shop at 2 Sheep Street, Bicester, in c1893. Back row, left to right: Sarah Etheldreda (1875-1942), Robert James (1871-1950), seedsman, of the Isle of Wight, Annie Wilhelmina (1866-1944), Frederick William (1868-1915), coal merchant, of Bicester, Louise Mary (1873-?), George (1877-1960), greengrocer, of 2 Sheep Street, and May Ellison. Centre row, left to right: Emily Elizabeth Goble (1864-?), matron of the workhouse on the Isle of Wight, William Wain Goble and his wife Mary Ellison, née Bennett, and Edward Charles Goble (1862-1952), florist and seedsman, of the Isle of Wight. Front row, left to right: Helen Septima (1885-?), known as Nellie, Richard Bennett (1883-1916), house agent, of 48 Sheep Street, and Winifred Decima (1881-?), known as Daisy. The second eldest daughter of William and Mary Goble, Annie Wilhelmina, married Robert Spencer Hudson of Rugby, who supervised the making of the Lutyens-designed dolls house for Queen Mary in 1923. Their son, Robert George Spencer Hudson (1895-1965), became Professor of Geology at Leeds University and was elected a member of the Royal Society in 1961. Through his extensive work on the Carboniferous period (he wrote more than 80 papers), the fossil coal measure Goniatite: Hudsonoceras (found in Ireland) was named after him. (Courtesy of William Hudson)

A window display at Hedges' drapers and outfitters' shop on Market Hill, c1902-1905 showing the latest women's fashions in the window on the left and a selection of men's shirts, caps and straw boaters in the window on the right. A youthful figure wearing spectacles, identified as Sid Hedges, author of *Bicester wuz a little town* (published in 1965), can just be seen standing behind the shop doorway. The light from outside the shop is reflected in his spectacles.

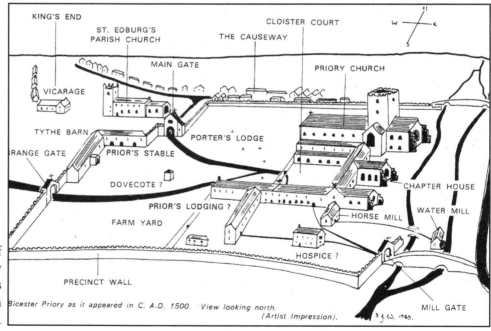

Bird's-eye view of Bicester Priory shortly before its dissolution in 1536.

Bicester Priory as it appeared in C. A.D. 1500. View looking north.
(Artist Impression).

The large priory church was demolished immediately but the cloister buildings survived until the 1670s, when they were demolished by Chief Justice Sir William Glynne to provide building material for his new house at Ambrosden. For many years the priory was the most important building in Bicester and was used by Henry VIII as a convenient location to discuss matters of government with officials. It also provided Elizabeth I with over-night accommodation when she came to stay with the Moore family in 1568.

Engraving from Alfred Rimmer's *Pleasant Spots around Oxford* (1878) showing the *Bowling Green* public house in Old Place Yard near the dovecote. The building backed on to the old cemetery wall of St Edburg's church and originally formed part of the stables of Bicester Priory. The inn took its name from the 18th century bowling green situated between the public house and the dovecote. The playing of bowls here appears to have continued a much earlier sporting tradition on the site. Excavations of the priory in 1965 found several small stone balls about four inches in diameter which had been used by the monks to play an early form of bowls.

The Hospice le Bell now known as the *Old Priory* reproduced from John Dunkin's *History of Bicester and Alchester* published in 1816. The building still survives and is traditionally believed to have been the Hospice of the former Bicester Priory, whose conventual buildings

stood close nearby. The *Hospice* is mentioned in the priory's 1425 bursars' accounts and may have been rebuilt in the early 16th century. Following its possible use as a hospice the building seems to have become an inn known as the *Bell* rented from the priory by a female licensee.

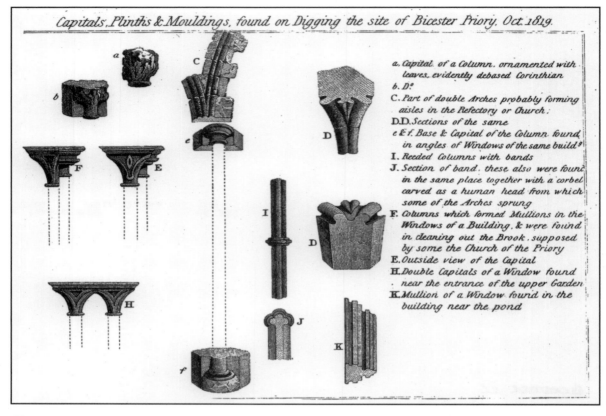

Capitals, Plinths & Mouldings, found on Digging the site of Bicester Priory. Oct. 1819.

a. Capital. of a Column. ornamented with leaves, evidently debased Corinthian
b. D°.
C. Part of double Arches probably forming aisles in the Refectory or Church.
D.D. Sections of the same
e & f. Base & Capital of the Column found in angles of Windows of the same build⁸
I. Reeded Columns with bands
J. Section of band. these also were found in the same place together with a corbel carved as a human head from which some of the Arches sprung
F. Columns which formed Mullions in the Windows of a Building. & were found in cleaning out the Brook. supposed by some the Church of the Priory
E. Outside view of the Capital
H. Double Capitals of a Window found near the entrance of the upper Garden
K. Mullion of a Window found in the building near the pond

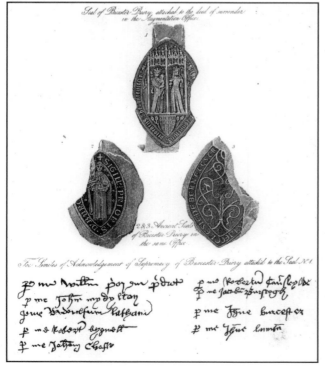

Carved mouldings and stonework found by John Dunkin in his 1819 excavations on the site of the cloister and the east end of Bicester Priory church, illustrated in his *History of the Bullingdon and Ploughley Hundreds*, published 1823. Some of the stone used for additions to the priory in the 14th century was ironstone brought from Deddington Castle following its demolition by Edward II after the Gaveston affair. Piers Gaveston was held by the King's enemies in Deddington Castle, after which the king took his revenge on them by demolishing the castle.

Document written in 1534 carrying the seal of Bicester Priory and the signatures of the prior and eight canons. The priory was dissolved two years later in 1536 and the prior and canons pensioned off. Part of the priory estates were bought by the King's brother-in-law, Charles Brandon, Duke of Suffolk, who sold them in 1542 making a considerable profit.

Charles Brandon, Duke of Suffolk, with his wife Mary, née Tudor, the favourite sister of Henry VIII. The King named his ill-fated warship, the *Mary Rose* after her. On Mary's death Charles married Catherine Willoughby, who like Flora Thompson was descended from the Norman family of Becke, which had a lordship at Eresby, Lincolnshire. (Courtesy of Patrick and Judith Phillips, Kentwell Hall, Suffolk)

The Shrine of St Edburg probably the work of Alexander of Abingdon, was removed to Stanton Harcourt church when Bicester's priory church was demolished in 1536. The shrine was saved from the destruction along with a few other sculpted items by Sir Simon Harcourt, the Sheriff of Oxfordshire, who superintended the demolition. The top section of the shrine is made of Purbeck marble and the bottom section of Oolitic limestone.

The painted Purbeck marble canopy of the Shrine of St Edburg carrying the sculptured heads of the Plantagenet family and their coats of arms. Among the heraldic arms represented are those of Bicester Priory (*wavy, argent and sable*), Eleanor of Provence, the wife of Henry III (*or, three pallets gules*), William Longespée, Earl of Salisbury and Lord of Bicester (*azure six lioncels or*) and Thomas, Earl of Lancaster, executed in 1322 (*England with a label of France*). It is believed that the shrine and its encompassing tiled floor decorated with heraldic motifs were a gift to the priory from the Earl of Lancaster following his marriage to Alice de Lacy, the daughter of Henry de Lacy, Earl of Lincoln, and great-grand-daughter of William Longespée, first Earl of Salisbury.

Tiles from the floor which is thought to have surrounded the shrine of St Edburg at Bicester. Some of the tiles are embossed with the double-headed eagle, the heraldic device of Richard, Earl of Cornwall (a younger brother of Henry III), when he became King of the Romans. Other tiles carry the royal lions of England and fleur-de-lys of France.

BUCKNELL

Bucknell is named from 'Bucca's Hill', after an Anglo-Saxon settler. There were two settlements in the parish in the middle ages: Bucknell and the now lost hamlet of Saxenton. The Damory family, who probably acquired the manor from Robert d'Oilly in the late 11th century, built a large moated manor house. Members of the family held important local positions such as Sheriff of Oxfordshire and Constable of Oxford Castle in the 13th and 14th centuries.

In 1652 Samuel Trotman took over the manor, which had been mortgaged to him by Francis Ewer, when Francis was unable to pay him. A second manor house built in the 17th century was partially replaced by the present one, built by Lenthall Trotman, lord of the manor 1685-1710. Lenthall was named after Speaker Lenthall, an uncle of Samuel's second wife, suggesting that the Trotmans were Parliamentarian. A 16th century plaster ceiling preserved in one bedroom has roundels containing heads such as Julius Caesar, Fama, Proserpine, Bellona and Joshua. A new wing was added in 1830 by lessee Thomas Tyrwhitt-Drake with more additions late in the century. During the Second World War the house was used by the BBC and in 1949 became an old people's home.

The only other substantial building was the Old Rectory, built around 1600, which had 48 bays including outbuildings. It was given new windows and divided in half in the 18th century, with half used for visiting rectors (they were mostly non-resident) and the other half used by the glebe farmer. It was partially demolished and rebuilt in the 19th century. When the hearth tax was calculated in 1665, apart from the manor house and the rectory, there were fourteeen dwellings, thirteen of which had only one hearth. Later there were three farms and a smithy was built by the Trigger Pond. The *Trigger Pond Inn* is an old stone building, but was not used as an inn until the end of the 19th century, as the Trotmans had refused to countenance an inn in the village on the grounds that it would encourage drunkenness.

Bucknell was closely associated with the Bicester Hunt: Samuel Trotman, squire from 1751 to 1775, kept a pack of hounds and T. Tyrwhitt-Drake, who was Master of the Bicester Hunt, brought the hunt kennels to Bucknell. The Bicester horse races took place here too on Bucknell Cow Common until it was enclosed in 1780.

Morris dancing was a good source of income for some labourers in the 19th century. In 1826 William Rolph (or Rolfe) was arrested in Oxford two days before Whit Monday, the traditional dancing season, for stealing twelve yards of ribbon, presumably for use by the morris men. He would have missed the dancing that year as he was imprisoned. The dancers went round quite a wide circuit including Middleton Cheney and often participated at the Kirtlington Lamb Ale Feast. Dancing came to a halt around 1863 but was revived in the 1870s, dying out again in the 1880s, although there were special performances for Queen Victoria's jubilees in 1887 and 1897.

Bucknell, Bicester.

A picturesque view of the centre of Bucknell taken by Mountain for French, the stationer, of Bicester, in 1907.

The church of St Peter, Bucknell, photographed for French in c1905. The church is considered to be a fine example of 13th century architecture, although the tower located between the chancel and nave belongs to an earlier church built in the 11th and 12th centuries. The north, south and east walls of the chancel have their original lancet windows. Behind the church stands the manor house of Bucknell manor, which is believed to be in part 17th century with later additions. The present structure stands on the site of a moated medieval manor house,

which was probably built by Richard Damory, Lord of Bucknell, who was a regular visitor to Bicester Priory. In the 1665 hearth tax the manor house was assessed on nineteen hearths, which suggests that the original medieval building was of very large proportions.

Bucknell's only public house, *The Trigger Pond*, as seen in the 1930s. From 1933 to 1947, the premises operated as an off-licence, run by Mr Frank Powell. In July 1947 the brewers, Halls Oxford Brewery, secured a full licence for the property and the pub became known as *The Trigger Pond*. Mrs Irene Prentice, Mr Powell's daughter, reported that the original intention was to name the premises The *Twigger Pond*, because the local gypsies frequently camped around the nearby pond making clothes pegs from local twigs; however, owing to opposition from the brewery, the proposed name of *Twigger* was abandoned in favour of *Trigger*. The Powell family gave up the tenancy in 1959.

A gypsy with her child selling clothes pegs in c1910. Gypsies regularly perambulated the area between Bicester, Banbury and Buckingham until the 1950s, selling wooden clothes pegs and flowers made from red crêpe paper.

Pig Row, also known as New Row, Bucknell, in 1910. On the evening of 8 July 1947, the thatched roof caught fire and several of the cottages were completely gutted. Before eight fire appliances arrived from Bicester, Buckingham and Brackley local residents rescued a large quantity of furniture and formed a chain gang with buckets in an attempt to save the cottages. Several families lost their homes, including the Prentice family.

Bucknell's morris dancers wearing top hats with their taborer, Joseph Powell, in about 1882. Joseph Powell lived in Bucknell from c1846 to 1937 and is credited by the *Victoria County History* as having been the last traditional pipe and tabor player in England. Bucknell still retains a strong morris dancing group and the music to several well-known dances, such as *the Princess Royal* and *the Blue Eyed Stranger* and the jigs *Bonnets so Blue* and *Shepherd's Hey*, was collected here and taken down in the early 1900s.

Bucknell morris dancers outside Harris Morgan's photographer's shop on Bicester Market Square in the early 1960s. (Courtesy of Michael Morgan)

Maypole dancing at Bucknell in c1905. Many of the girls wear smock dresses.

MIDDLETON STONEY

The village has been greatly influenced by two families, the de Camvilles and the Villiers. The castle was probably built around 1130-50 by the notable de Camville family, who came from Canville-les-Deux-Eglises in Normandy and also held a castle at Lilburne in Northamptonshire. Richard de Camville was prominent in the reign of King Stephen, witnessing sixty-three charters for him as well as the peace treaty at Westminster negotiated between Stephen and the future Henry II. He was later entrusted with escorting Henry II's daughter Joan to Palermo in 1176-7 to marry William II of Sicily, dying en route. His son Gerard was also prominent, becoming castellan of Lincoln castle and holding sixteen knights fees through his marriage to heiress Nicola de Hay.

Gerard supported King John during his struggles with Richard I, to the extent that he was temporarily deprived of his castles by King Richard, being compelled to pay 2000 marks to regain Middleton, so it is not surprising that John rewarded him in 1201 with a licence to empark (and the gift of ten bucks and 40 does from Woodstock Park, followed by more gifts of deer over the years) and the grant of a two-day market at Middleton Stoney. This indicated a desire to establish a town, and traces of this are indicated by the Hundred Rolls of 1279, which mention burgage holders, and long strips north of the castle which may be the remains of burgage plots. A second market and annual fair were granted in 1294. However, the ravages of the Black Death ended the urban venture. Gerard exerted influence locally, purchasing from King John the wardship of Eustasia, daughter of Gilbert Basset, lord of Bicester and Baron of Headington and marrying her to his son Richard.

However, Gerard's son Richard rebelled against King John and was punished by having Middleton castle demolished in 1215 (never to be rebuilt) and his heiress Idonea was held at Corfe Castle by the King, who granted her wardship to William Longespée, who married her to his son William, second Earl of Salisbury. William was killed crusading in Palestine in 1250 and buried in Salisbury Cathedral. Their son William died in 1257 from injuries sustained in a tournament, but their grand-daughter Alice de Lacy married Thomas, Earl of Lancaster, cousin of the King, and Lancaster presented the shrine of St Edburg to Bicester Priory around 1310.

William Villiers, third Earl of Jersey, purchased the manor in 1737 for £6000, acquiring more lands for £20,000 until he owned almost the entire parish. His grandson George Child-Villiers (1773-1859), the fifth Earl, had a reputation as a superb rider, described by 'Nimrod' as *'the boldest, most judicious, and perhaps the most elegant rider to hounds whom the world ever saw'*, and Middleton became celebrated for its stables, where he bred racehorses, and its kennels. He had a Derby winner in 1825 and bred the famous *Bay Middleton* in 1833. He twice served as Master of the Horse to Queen Victoria.

The 5th Earl increased the size of his park to occupy about half the village, demolishing several cottages in 1824-5. His wife, Sarah Sophia, the daughter of John Fane, the 10th Earl of Westmorland, and his wife Sarah Anne Child, daughter of the banking magnate Robert Child, despite being a pillar of society (including being a patroness of the prestigious Almack's Assembly Rooms, director of Child's Bank and owner of Osterley Park), took a great personal interest in the village, organising picturesque replacement cottages with porches and flower gardens. She set up three schools in the village, one where 30 young girls were taught reading and writing, another for 20-30 boys who learnt reading and writing and how to do odd jobs, and a school where girls spent three or four years training to be domestic servants, learning reading, writing, arithmetic, sewing and housework. In her will she left money to provide four almshouse cottages built by her husband.

Sir Victor Albert George Child-Villiers (1845-1915), the 7th Earl, was also a benevolent landowner, establishing a village reading room, improving the water supply, extending the schools and setting up cricket and football pitches.

Middleton Stoney remained the principal family seat of the Earls of Jersey until 1946 when the house and estate were sold to A.C.J. Wall.

The centre of Middleton Stoney village near the *Jersey Arms* public house. Parts of the building have been dated by dendrochronology to the 13th century. James Blomfield of Launton recorded that conjoined twins were born in the house next to the *Jersey Arms* (formerly the Eagle) on 3 August 1552. They lived for sixteen days (*Diary of John Machyn, citizen of London* and Parish Register).

Richard Butler, better known locally as Sprucy Dick, driving Frederick Garrett's horse-drawn cart laden with boxes of lemonade manufactured at his farmhouse at Stud Farm, Middleton Stoney, in the 1890s. Garrett appears to have been licensee of the *White Hart* in Sheep Street, Bicester, from the late 1860s to c1880 where he operated a lemonade bottling plant behind the public house. He also seems to have been licensee of the *Fox and Hounds* at Ardley in the 1870s and the *Jersey Arms* at Middleton Stoney in about 1881. Several glass lemonade bottles carrying the inscription *F. R. Garrett* and the places of lemonade manufacture (Bicester, Ardley and Middleton Stoney) have been found and are often of two types. These are Codd's bottles made according to Hiram Codd's patent 246 (taken out in 1873) and the Codd/Hamilton Hybrid.

The 12th century motte of the de Camville family's castle in Middleton Stoney Park etched by J. and H.S. Storer from a sketch made by E. Williams in 1822.

The effigy of William Longespée, first Earl of Salisbury, who died in 1226, the first person to be buried in Salisbury Cathedral. He was the illegitimate son of Henry II and thus the half-brother of Kings Richard I and John. William's son, William Longespée II (died 1250), married Idonea de Camville of Middleton Stoney, the grand-daughter of Gilbert Basset, founder of Bicester Priory, and so William Longespée II, by the right of his wife, became Lord of Bicester.

The motte and bailey castle of the de Camville family at Middleton Stoney as seen today. The castle was built in the 12th century and occupied the site of a building belonging to a Roman villa. The tower of the Norman parish church which can be seen beyond the remains of the motte is all that survives of the village demolished in the 19th century by the Earl of Jersey, which once stood west of the castle.

The font in Middleton Stoney church in which King Edward the Confessor was baptised in about 1004 A.D. according to local tradition. The font is held to have come from the Anglo-Saxon chapel at Islip, which stood near Islip church until the 18th century. In its present form the font dates to the 14th century but it may have been reworked from an earlier Anglo-Saxon tub font. The outside of the font bears a curious inscription:

Let this remayne
The Trophee of his fame
A king baptized
From hence a saint became

This sacred font St Edward first
Received from wombe to grace went
His virtuous life to this fayre isle
Bequeathed Pease and to us but lent

(Courtesy of Michael Morgan)

Engraving of the mansion built in the late 1750s at Middleton Stoney and later enlarged 1806-1807 for the 5th Earl of Jersey. It replaced an earlier structure destroyed by a fire on 3rd May 1753, which was started when a housemaid aired linen too close to a fire. This building was in turn demolished in 1938 to make way for the present house designed by Sir Edwin Lutyens. The drawing was sketched by E. Williams and etched by J. and H.S. Storer in 1822.

The dining room of the 18th century Middleton Stoney Park house, photographed by Bicester chemist J. T. Mountain for W.J. French, the postmaster and stationer of Bicester in 1910. The photograph suggests that one end of the dining-room ceiling was supported on two free-standing Ionic columns. Several large 17th century portraits of the Villiers family can be seen decorating the walls.

The crowning of Miss Joan Grace as Carnival Queen by Lady Jersey, formerly Virginia Cherrill (star of the silent film *City Lights* with Charlie Chaplin in 1931), on Bicester Sports Ground on 1 August 1938. Before her marriage to the 9th Earl of Jersey in 1937, Virginia Cherrill (1908-1996) was the wife of the well-known actor, Cary Grant. (Courtesy of Harris Morgan)

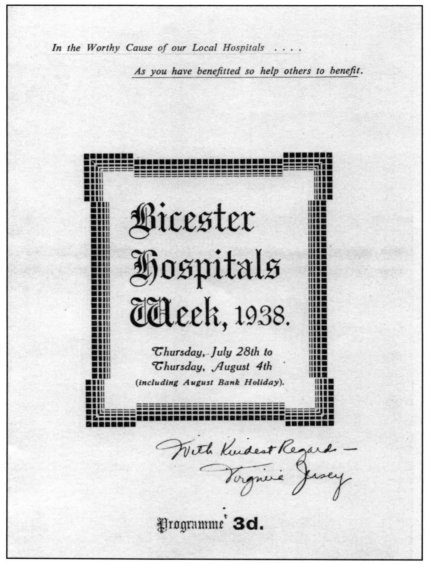

Front of the programme for the Bicester Hospitals week, held from Thursday 28 July to Thursday 4 August 1938, signed by Virginia Cherrill, Lady Jersey. The week of festivities raised funds for the Bicester Cottage Hospital and Oxford's Radcliffe Infirmary, Eye Hospital and the Wingfield Orthopaedic Hospital. The main event of the week was the crowning of the Carnival Queen by the Countess of Jersey at 2 p.m. on Carnival day on the Bank Holiday Monday. So many people were expected to attend that people were advised to get to Bicester Sports Ground early to witness the 'Crowning and the Opening Ceremony'. In order to be chosen Carnival Queen, candidates had to canvass votes from local villagers and townspeople, who each paid one penny to vote. The programme records that Miss Joan Grace won the contest with 4022 votes and was chosen Carnival Queen. Miss Marjorie Taylor came second with 2794 votes and was made Maid of Honour.

FROM ARDLEY TO MIXBURY

Ardley

Emma Dibber, Flora Thompson's mother, was born in Ardley in 1853 and was brought up in a cottage near the church. Emma's father John was described in census returns as an agricultural labourer, although Flora describes him as an eggler, collecting eggs locally and taking them in his horse and cart to sell in the market town. He married Hannah Pollard, 'the belle of Hornton', in 1835, when the couple were respectively 21 and 19. John was a religious man, playing his violin in Ardley church band, but he later became a Methodist preacher and gave up playing the violin to travel round villages to preach. He and Hannah retired to Cottisford where he died in 1887 and Hannah went to Daventry to live with her son William.

Flora wrote that Emma was taken under the wing of the wife of Revd Lowe, the rector, but it must have been his sister-in-law Ann Hind, as his wife died young. Revd Lowe lived in the village for over 50 years, most of that time as rector and was much loved. Emma must have told Flora about him, as in *Lark Rise to Candleford* she described visiting him and being given a green patterned mug. However, this visit was invented, as he died in 1874 before Flora was born.

Emma became a nursemaid in the next-door village of Fewcott (now part of Ardley), where she worked for the Revd Joscelyne, the curate, tending his seven children, the oldest of whom, Louise Elizabeth, was only four years younger than Emma, so she was able to be more like an elder sister and the children loved her.

It must have been quite a shock for the quiet village when a temporary navvy village was constructed for labourers building the nearby railway tunnel. Whole families lived there, not just the workers, and the inhabitants were listed in census returns. Attendance at services could number up to 200, mostly men, and the children attended Sunday School from 11-3. Women could take technical dressmaking classes and excursions were organised in the summer. The Revd Meredith wrote in 1909 about the work going on at the mission and the need for £321 each year to support its activities for the next three years:

A visit to the works would bring home to the mind the great need there is of such a mission, as the ordinary parochial agencies are unable to cope with such a large influx of men and their families as the works bring with them. The other day the Vicar paid a visit to the settlement at Ardley, and was conducted round the huts by Mr Eglington, the missioner. It comprises quite a small village consisting of four lines of huts and the mission room at the end is a bright building… Besides being used for services it is also used as a recreation and reading room, and concerts from time to time are also held in it. There are also cricket and football clubs for the men and lads, and a sick club and a band of hope. Also there is a Sunday School for the children, attended by between sixty and seventy. Besides the services on Sunday there is a week night service. This is not intended to be a full list ... but it will give some idea of the work, which is being done... It is highly interesting to watch the actual work on the railway itself, with the steam navvies, etc, and one can see how hard and dangerous the work is unless great care is taken, and the enormous amount of trouble which is entailed before a railway is ready to use.

In 1925 part of the parish was separated to form the RAF Upper Heyford air force base, which was later used by the American Air Force and has now been decommissioned.

Stoke Lyne

The village's name derives from the Old English *'stoc'* or cattle farm. It was originally termed Stoke Insula, perhaps because the lowlands round the village tended to flood, then Stoke Lisle after the medieval lords of the manor, which was changed to Stoke Lyne when the Lynde or Lyne family took on that role in the fifteenth century. Minor settlements in the parish were Bainton and Fewcott (the latter now part of Ardley parish).

Woodland in the parish called *'Fethelee'* may have been the site of an Anglo-Saxon battle of 'Fethanleag', fought in 584 between Ceawlin, King of the West Saxons, and the native Britons, but an alternative site has been suggested in the Severn valley. Bayard's Green (now Baynard's), situated in the north of the parish, which has a large open area, was probably the site of 13th century tournaments and was later used by Charles I's army in 1644 and before the battle of Naseby in 1645. There are references to a six-mile horse-racing track in the 17th century.

A manor house was probably built by William Lyne in the 15th century. In the 17th century Charnel Petty lived there and his notable cousin, Anthony Wood, the historian and antiquary, visited frequently. The house had ten hearths in the 1660s but was demolished in the early 19th century.

Sir Thomas Mostyn bought Bainton Manor Farm around the end of the 18th century from John Warde, a prominent Master of the Bicester hunt, who had built stables and kennels there. Sir Thomas took over as Master in 1800 and it was renamed the Bicester and Warden Hill hunt. Nimrod wrote that *'there are few better qualified to be at the head of a pack of foxhounds than Sir Thomas, his attention to his kennels is great, and in the field he is a pattern for all Masters.'* He began selective hound breeding and built and moved to Swift's House in Bainton. A later Master was Sir Henry Peyton, who built the school in 1858 and after whom the public house was renamed from *The Royal George* to *The Peyton Arms*.

Kezia Kirby, the major inspiration for the character of Flora Thompson's *Miss Lane*, the postmistress, was born in Stoke Lyne on 11 January 1835. She was a daughter of Alexander Kirby, a farmer and blacksmith (born in Fritwell) and his wife Elizabeth, née Bayliss.Their other children who survived to adulthood were George (born in 1820), Mary Ann (born in 1822) and Louisa (born in 1833). Alexander died in 1864 and was buried in the village. Kezia probably lived here until she married John Whitton in 1857 and they moved to Fringford to run the forge there.

There was a morris dance team in the village from about the 1840s to the 1860s or 1870s, which performed at the Friendly Society feasts. Team members included Edmund and Walter Heydon, Levi and James James, William Jaycock and Edward Timms.

Souldern

Early Anglo-Saxon remains have been found in Souldern, including a fine decorated bucket now housed in the Ashmolean Museum. No traces of the Anglo-Saxons remain in the present village, but it retained importance in the middle ages, being one of the wealthiest locally. In 1279 it was described as a privileged manor, its lords enjoying free warren, waif, view of frankpledge and freedom from suit of hundred. It was held by Thomas de Lewknor from Thomas de Arderne for the unusual rent of a pound of cumin per year. A strange tale is attached to rector John Barnewell, who died in 1305, who apparently abducted the daughter of the lord of the manor, though why he did it is uncertain.

Souldern's prosperity must have continued into the 17th century and is attested by the number of fine mellow Oxfordshire stone buildings, including the manor house, remaining from this period. An unusual number of trades were recorded then, including tailors and a mercer, weaver, smith, carpenter and mason. Cheese manufacture became a local speciality.

The principal women's craft in the first half of the 19th century was lacemaking. At one time there were three lace schools in the village and in 1851 there were thirty-six girls and women making lace, varying in age from eight to sixty-two. The number of girls involved showed that the industry was still strong, but shortly after this it began to decline after the invention of machine-made lace.

Flora Thompson's nephew Leslie Castle lived in Souldern and they struck up a strong bond. Although Flora never visited him, he often stayed with her in Devon and Flora's letters to him reveal clues about her books. For example, he told her about the church rhyme '*Adderbury for length, Bloxham for strength and Kings Sutton for beauty*' and Flora decided to use it in *Still Glides the Stream* to draw a red herring over where she was really writing about. She told Leslie how much she would have liked to have visited both Souldern and Ardley, where her mother was born.

Somerton

Somerton, which also has Saxon origins, was one of the largest and wealthiest medieval villages in the Ploughley Hundred, declining in the second half of the 19th century. The 1660 hearth tax recorded eleven substantial houses, including the 22-hearth manor house, built by William Fermor, clerk of the King's Bench and son of a wealthy Witney clothier. It fell into ruin and only a fragment of the hall remains. Richard Fermor purchased Tusmore in 1606 and this became the principal family residence, but the grand tombs of the early Fermors can be seen in Somerton church. The Fermors were Catholic and encouraged a strong local Catholic community until they sold the manor in 1852 to the Earl of Jersey.

May Day has been strongly celebrated here, and the garland, like the one at Cottisford described by Flora Thompson, features a doll, which was believed locally, because of the Catholic connection, to represent the Virgin Mary. The doll, which has a composition face and blonde painted hair, has been used in the garland since the Victorian era. She was given a new long white silk dress with a blue sash and a red velvet cloak in 1953. The Lord and Lady who headed the procession in 1903 later became May King and Queen and the procession included two boys bearing a staff and banner and two boys carrying the garland, followed by the other children.

Mixbury

A small round barrow forms the earliest visible remains here. The small village, which originated in the Anglo-Saxon period, runs along the course of a stream, with the church isolated apart from the banks and ditches which are the only remains of Beaumont Castle, probably built by the Norman lord Roger d'Ivry. The village was relatively wealthy and may have been the chief seat of the family. Excavations have revealed remains of a dungeon or well and an underground passage. The open ground between the village and Brackley formed part of the tournament ground of Bayard's Green. The hamlet of Fulwell had a medieval mill and grange belonging to Oseney Abbey.

In 1851 nearly all the men worked as agricultural labourers and there was a high degree of poverty with several people recorded as claiming parish relief as their only source of income. Trades included blacksmiths Henry Kirby from Fritwell and Robert Kirby from Mixbury (who may have been related to Kezia Whitton, née Kirby, Flora's *Miss Lane*), a farrier, carrier, gamekeeper, woodman, sawyer, four tailors, a dressmaker, baker, grocer, carter, four shepherds, six lacemakers and several servants. The vicar had the most servants, employing a footman, cook, housemaid and general servant. The nine carpenters were mostly from the

Finch family – a surname used by Flora for her heroine *Charity Finch* in *Still Glides the Stream*.

Many of the cottages which dominate the village street were rebuilt in 1874 when the Court of Chancery ordered that dilapidated cottages should be replaced by forty odd semi-detached houses with brick quoins.

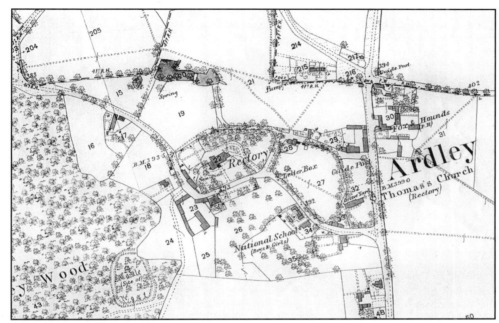

Ordnance Survey map of Ardley Village published in 1881. The site of the 12th century medieval moated castle can be seen bottom left. Its precincts may once have contained Ardley's medieval manor-house.

The 17th century rectory at Ardley. The Revd John Lowe was the vicar here when Emma Dibber, Flora Thompson's mother, was a girl. (Courtesy of Oxfordshire County Council Photographic Archive)

The digging of the Great Western Railway cutting between Ardley and Bucknell in 1908. The ground was excavated with a steam navvy and the spoil drawn away in a horse-drawn rail wagon to build the embankment further down the line between Bucknell and Bicester.

The building of the Ardley Tunnel on the Great Western line, three miles north of Bucknell near Ardley in 1908. Above the newly-built tunnel can be seen the outline of the huts which once accommodated the navvies of the Railway mission village. A similar village was located further down the line at Ludgershall. (Courtesy of John Jackson)

The interior of a Navvy mission chapel similar to those built at Ardley and Ludgershall.

Oolitic limestones of the Jurassic period exposed in Ardley Quarry two miles north-west of Bucknell near the former Great Western railway line in 1969. In 2001 a surprise discovery was made here of dozens of footprints left by two species of land-based dinosaurs. These were the meat-eating Megalosaurs and the plant-eating Sauropods. Both species had been walking, and in some cases running, in shallow water on the edge of the Jurassic Sea some 160 million years ago. It has been suggested that the footprints may have been preserved in Jurassic times by a storm which suddenly caused large amounts of silt to be washed into the tracks, thus preserving their outline. Casts of the footprints are now on view at the University Museum in Oxford and in the dinosaur garden at the Oxfordshire Museum, Woodstock. In the 1940s, the vertebrae of another land-based dinosaur, the massively large Brontosaurus,

were found four miles from Ardley at Stratton Audley stone quarry on the northern perimeter of Bicester RAF station. The animal had been walking along the margins of the same shallow sea as the dinosaurs once living at Ardley.

Reconstruction of a Megalosaur dinosaur whose footprints were discovered at Ardley Quarry, which is displayed with its footprints in the Dinosaur Garden at the Oxfordshire Museum, Woodstock.

The former Rectory at Fewcott, adjacent to the old village school, where Emma Dibber worked as a nursemaid for the family of the Revd Henry Joscelyne. The house is now known as *Weavers*.

St Peter's parish church and Forge Cottage, Stoke Lyne. Flora Thompson's *Miss Lane*, in real life Kezia Kirby (the postmistress and blacksmith at *Candleford Green*), was born in the cottage in 1835. She was the youngest of the three daughters of the village blacksmith, Alexander Kirby, and his wife Elizabeth, née Bayliss. Kezia's father was buried in the cemetery opposite in 1864. The blacksmith's forge lay immediately east of the cottage and part of its back wall survives in the yard of the house next door, now known as Forge House. The greater part of the forge was demolished in about 1980. In the 19th century a large chestnut tree stood opposite the forge on the verge next to the wall of Stoke Lyne cemetery and gave useful shade in summer to horses waiting to be shod.

Members of the Stoke Lyne Friendly Society with the village band on club day, outside the *Peyton Arms* in about 1905. The young man in the centre playing a banjo is Rodney Denny. Others on the photograph have been identified as Joseph Beasley, John Coggins, Vincent Golder, Arthur James, Sir Algernon Peyton of Swifts House, Lewis Hickman, bailiff of the Swifts House estate, Thomas Harris, Fredrick Butler, Harry White, Alfred Richardson and Charles Brandrick.

A young farmhand rolling a field with a roller pulled by a team of two horses at Stoke Lyne in c1905. Rolling was often done in the spring to tighten the ground so that the newly sown corn would root better. It also served to press down surface stones, which helped to retain moisture in the ground.

Mangel-wurzels being lifted and carted away on the Swifts House estate, Stoke Lyne, c1905. They were used for animal food during the winter months, as still happens in Scotland.

The centre of Souldern Village in c1906. Flora Thompson knew the village as her nephew Leslie Castle (son of her sister May) lived there. During the 1940s Flora maintained an animated correspondence with Leslie Castle and several of these letters give further insight into the background of Flora's writing of *Lark Rise to Candleford*, which is frequently mentioned.

The Witherses' family home overlooking Souldern village pond in Souldern in 1903. At the instigation of his publisher, the well-known poet A.E.Housman, author of *A Shropshire Lad*, spent most of his summers with the Withers family at this house from 1922 to 1935. Housman enjoyed taking long walks in the countryside around Souldern and often used the isolation of his walks to compose poems based on the landscape.

Flora Thompson's nephew Leslie Castle, with whom she corresponded at the end of her life in the 1940s. (Courtesy of Henry Westbury)

St Mary's church, Somerton. The church contains the remains of ten generations of the Fermor family, the lords of the manor, who were buried here between 1552 and 1828.

ton Castle

All that is left of the former hall of Somerton manor house, demolished in the 18th century, is part of a stone wall containing a traceried window of two lights. The manor house, known to locals as 'the castle', was bought from the De Grey family in the early 16th century by William Fermor (the son of a Witney cloth merchant and himself a clerk of the King's Bench), whose family eventually moved to Tusmore in 1625. Following the departure of Henry Fermor, his brother's widow married Lord Arundel of Wardour and continued to live in the manor house at Somerton. During the reign of Charles II the Arundels twice entertained James, Duke of York, the future James II, here during periods when he was nationally very unpopular in the country. According to Nicholas Pevsner's *Oxfordshire* in the *Buildings of England* series, the manor house originally had a central dining hall with a parlour above and two flanking wings.

The Maze or Troy situated opposite Troy Farm, Somerton. It has low turf banks separated by gravel and may originally have been laid out in medieval times. There are now only seven turf mazes known in Britain and it has been argued that they may represent a legacy from the Roman occupation of Britain when Roman colonists cut them to play the Troy game of *Lusus Trojae.* The Roman historian, Pliny the younger, writing in the first century A.D., mentions that sometimes mazes were laid out in fields or in mosaic pavements specially for the purpose of entertaining children. Ethel Carlton Williams writing in her *Companion into Oxfordshire* (1935) maintains that *Turf Mazes have survived because in the Middle Ages they were used for village games. Treading the maze was a favourite amusement for many generations, and was evidently known to Shakespeare. The sight of this strange ramification of lines ...recalls one of the loveliest scenes in* **A Midsummer Night's Dream** *when Titania reproaches Oberon and speaking of the wet summer says:*

> *"The quaint mazes in the wanton green*
> *For lack of tread are indistinguishable."*

In medieval times the turf banks may have been followed from the outside to the centre of the maze by religious penitents, walking on hands and knees saying prayers. Mazes of one kind and another are found throughout England and also in French cathedrals.

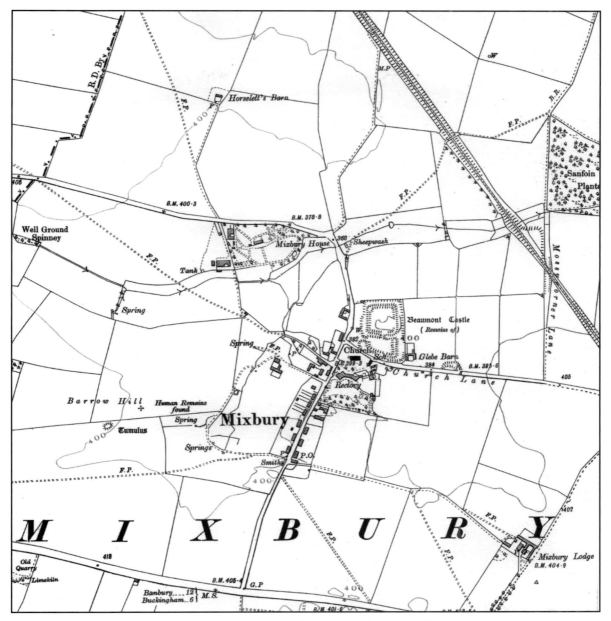

Ordnance Survey map showing the village of Mixbury in 1900. The site of Beaumont Castle can be seen north of the church.

The main street of Mixbury in 1905, which contains some 40 semi-detached houses, built of rubble with red brick dressings. The model village replaced existing old cottages and was created in 1874 by order of the Court of Chancery. The original houses were little more than slum dwellings and Blomfield describes them as huts *'with here and there an upper room reached by a ladder'*. According to the *Victoria County History of Oxfordshire*, Vol. VI, many of the 'huts' had chimneys constructed of wood.

The west tower of All Saints Church, Mixbury, built in the 15th century. The tower is almost all that survives of the original church, which was largely re-built in the 1840s using existing old windows and mouldings. The south doorway with zig-zag ornament dates from c1170. North-east of the church (across the road leading to Fulwell) are the remains of the enormous circuit ditch, rampart and stone foundations of Beaumont Castle. The castle was built by Roger d'Ivry in c1070 and may have served as the Caput to his barony. Later the castle belonged to the Bassets for a short time, before passing to the St Valery family. Excavations conducted in the 1950s found a deep dungeon or well at the north-west corner of the rampart and an underground passage leading to it.

Mixbury Rectory, built by the incumbent W. J. Palmer between 1802 and 1805, and enlarged in 1855. Palmer obtained a licence to rebuild the existing 17th century rectory from the Bishops of Oxford and Rochester and raised a loan of £390 with which to build it.

Ernest Alfred Watts (1878-1969), gentleman farmer of Waterloo Farm, Fringford and Monks House Farm, Mixbury, with his pet spaniel. Ernest and his sister Beatrice were two of the last members of the Watts family of farmers, who lived in the 19th and 20th centuries at Monks House and Fulwell Farm at Mixbury. Many of the family were buried at Hethe and several of their gravestones can be seen immediately outside the porch of the parish church. The census suggests that a number of labourers walked daily from the hamlet of Juniper, across the fields, to work on the Monks House Farm. Monks House and the nearby Knights House are two locations mentioned by Flora Thompson as childhood memories in her letters.

TUSMORE PARK

Tusmore's name has romantic connotations, being derived either from 'Thur's Pool' or 'a lake haunted by a giant or a demon'. The small village was one of the few totally destroyed by the Black Death of 1348-50 so in 1358 Sir Roger de Cotesford enclosed it as a park. Traces of the deserted medieval village are visible in a field near the cricket pitch. The Fermor family of Somerton, who purchased the manor in 1606, moving to Tusmore in about 1625, held the estate for seven generations. They were prominent Catholics with a chapel in the house served by a resident priest. Arabella Fermor, a noted 18th century society beauty, gained unwanted notoriety when she featured in Alexander Pope's poem *The Rape of the Lock*: she was so angry that he issued a new edition with a note that the poem did not refer to her.

In 1852 the estate was purchased for £152,000 by Henry Howard, 2nd Earl of Effingham, whose principal seat was The Grange, Rotherham. He moved into the house built by William Fermor to the designs of Robert Mylne. Although the building was finished by 1770, it took nine more years to complete the interior decoration and lay out the gardens (which included a Temple of Peace dedicated to Pope, so Arabella must have forgiven him!). The Earl built an additional wing and made other alterations.

The world of the people living at Tusmore Park was a world away from that of the villagers. Flora Thompson knew Tusmore as her local 'great house'. The Earl employed many farm labourers and exerted great influence locally. She referred to a beaded footstool kept in a cupboard of the cottage her family rented which belonged to the owner, who had retrieved it when Tusmore was damaged by fire. She offered it to Flora's mother Emma, who refused it.

The Earl only lived at the house for part of the year, as he also owned The Grange and a house in Eaton Place, London. Many servants travelled with him and a skeleton staff was left when the family was not in residence: in 1881 the family were in London, and the only servants were three laundry maids, two housemaids, a dairymaid, a house porter and a gardener, presumably overseen by an estate manager. It was a different story when the family were in residence. In 1871 the Earl was at Tusmore with his wife Eliza, their adult daughters Lady Maria and Lady Alice, and grandson Henry Alexander Gordon Howard. They had a butler and housekeeper (unusually a married couple), cook, two ladies' maids, three housemaids, kitchen maid, scullery maid, four laundry maids, still room maid and dairymaid. The male servants were a coachman, two footmen and a page. Interestingly, none were recruited locally, perhaps to prevent local gossip about the family.

The current house, designed by Sir William Whitfield, was built recently as a Palladian villa, using superb craftsmanship, for Mr Wafic Said, a Syrian businessman and philanthropist, who financed the Said Business School in Oxford. Its grandeur is much more suited to the site than the small 1960s house it replaced. It has fittingly been described as *'perhaps the finest country house built since the Second World War.'* It cost £300 million, and was awarded the 2004 Georgian Architectural Award.

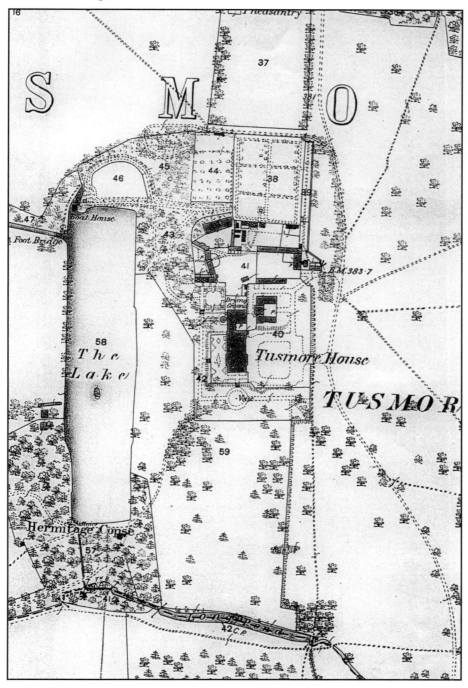

Ordnance Survey map surveyed in 1880 showing the house, lake and pleasure grounds designed and constructed for William Fermor by the architect Robert Mylne (1734-1811) in the 1770s. Mylne is perhaps best known for having designed Blackfriars Bridge across the Thames in London.

The main front of Tusmore House as created for William Fermor in the 1770s. The Italianate house was modified in the Victorian era with the addition of the 'barrack block' by the 2nd Earl of Effingham, built on the site of the chapel of the former medieval and 17th century manor house. William Fermor's house remained standing until about 1961 when it was demolished by the City of London financier, Vivian Smith, Lord Bicester, to make way for a low-level two-storied structure designed by Claud Phillimore.

The saloon on the first floor of Tusmore House as it appeared in the time of Henry Alexander Gordon Howard, 4th Earl of Effingham (c1906). The saloon was the focal point of the house and all the principal rooms on the first floor opened on to it. On the right can be seen a bust of the Roman Emperor Augustus standing on a green marble pedestal and (in the showcase opposite) the saddlecloth of crimson velvet and gold, and bridle and other trappings of the horse ridden by Kenneth Alexander Howard, first Earl of Effingham, acting Earl Marshal, at the coronation of George IV. The room was panelled in old oak (possibly reused from the earlier Tusmore House) and contained a piece of timber and an iron chest taken from one of the wrecked ships of the Spanish Armada.

The drawing-room walls of Tusmore House adorned with portrait and landscape paintings in 1905. The large portrait visible on the wall at the far end may be that of Lord Howard of Effingham, Lord High Admiral and Commander of the English fleet against the Spanish Armada, painted by Zucchero. The ceiling was painted by Angelica Kauffman and represented *the Amours of the Gods*. Mrs Fitzherbert was frequently an honoured guest at Tusmore in the 1790s and the Launton rector the Revd James C. Blomfield, recorded a local tradition (Tusmore, p.83) that George IV married Mrs Fitzherbert in the drawing-room seen here.

Miss Coleman of Church Villa, Bicester, with her sister, walking in the formal garden at the rear of Tusmore House in 1931. They were part of an invited group from St Edburg's church led by the vicar of Bicester, the Revd Walter O'Reilly.

The 4th Earl of Effingham, centre, riding with two grooms on the gravel drive at Tusmore House in about 1905. The stables, one of two sets, lay immediately behind the photographer.

A group of 'indoor' servants standing in the yard at the back of Tusmore House in c1905. From left to right, the men are believed to be: Joseph Walby, the Earl of Effingham's game-keeper; Mr Rouse, the Earl's footman; John Allen, brother of the Earl's land steward; Richard Allen, an under-footman; the Earl of Effingham's groom; and an unknown person.

The Earl of Effingham's 'outdoor' servants, enjoying themselves with a barrel of beer (brewed by Hall's Oxford Brewery) in the stable yard at Tusmore in c1905. On the far left, standing and wearing an apron, is Aloysius Harris, who worked as the Tusmore estate carpenter and in the 1880s lived at the Fox, Juniper. On his retirement he bought the Round House in Hethe and built the organ for Hardwick church. The man third from the right at the back, wearing a straw hat and holding a Doulton jug, is Charles James, the gardener and bee-keeper at Tusmore, who wrote several books on bee-keeping. Next to him and second from the right, holding a bottle, is Mr Hitchman, another Tusmore gardener. In front, squatting down and wearing a straw boater, is John Allen, licensee of the King's Head at Fritwell. According to John's great-nephew, the late Gordon Allen of Cottisford, John kept the servants at Tusmore supplied with a regular supply of beer and made his fortune by selling beer to the Irish navvies building the Great Western Railway near Ardley.

A shooting party made up of gamekeepers, beaters and household staff on the Tusmore estate in about 1905. The man on the left at the back, behind the beaters, wearing a high starched collar and tweed cap is Henry Alexander Howard, 4th Earl of Effingham.

The front façade of the new Tusmore House designed by Sir William Whitfield for businessman and philanthropist, Mr Wafic Said. The house was built in 2000 to 2002, and was one of the winners of the 2004 Georgian Group Architecture Awards. It stands on gently rising ground, which has been deliberately banked up on the eastern side to partially conceal two flanking pavilions, one of which accommodates the estate's offices. The building is faced with a dazzling white Ashlar limestone known as Massangis, which was specially quarried for the building at Dijon in Burgundy. The triangular pediment is supported on six free-standing and four engaged Ionic

columns, which rise to a height of a little over ten metres. The methods used in the building's construction are reminiscent of those used in Imperial Rome's monumental buildings, which were faced with white Carrara marble bonded into hidden brick and concrete.

The half-timbered granary and dovecote in the former farmyard at Tusmore is the only building to survive from the original medieval manor house complex. It is believed to have been constructed in the 15th century and is built of oak posts standing on stone foundation supports. The building has three floors with the ground and first floors being used as a granary, and the second floor as a dovecote.

The rear façade of the new Tusmore House with large Venetian windows at first floor level and French windows on the ground floor which open on to a wide expanse of lawn over-looking the lake.

Detail showing the entablature and some of the Ionic capitals of the six free-standing and four engaged columns which support the pediment over the east-facing portico at Tusmore House.

The impressive ornamental wrought-iron gates on the approach road to the east side of the new Tusmore House. The double garage built in 1903 for the 4th Earl of Effingham can be seen in the middle distance on the left. Also visible is a surviving section of one of the avenues of trees,

which were planted in the 18th century and were a well-known feature of the Tusmore estate in the early 1900s.

The 'motor car house' built by Henry Howard for his new Panhard Levassor car at Tusmore. The garage could accommodate two vehicles and represents one of the earliest purpose-built 'motor car houses' in the country.

The Effingham Coat of Arms and the inscription *A.D. Motor House, MCMIII*, above the two wooden doors of the Earl of Effingham's garage at Tusmore.

Henry Alexander Gordon Howard, 4th Earl of Effingham (1866-1927), in a fur-cuffed coat standing with his Panhard Levassor car outside the front door of Tusmore House in c1905. The back wheels of the car seem to have been chain driven. The car is credited as having been the very first to have been seen in the area and drew large crowds when it first arrived at Tusmore.

The lake at Tusmore House with the classical bridge and Temple of Peace dedicated to Pope. Alexander Pope, the poet, was a frequent visitor to Tusmore and in about 1712, hearing that Lord Petrie had incensed Arabella Fermor by cutting off a lock of her hair without permission, wrote his well-known poem, *The Rape of the Lock*. R.M. Marshall in the book *Oxfordshire Byways* wrote that Pope spent his time at Tusmore '*dozing all day when the sweet wine was out,*' and '*making his verses chiefly in the night, to the distraction of the maid whose business it was to supply him with coffee to keep him awake.*'

The lake covers more than eight acres and seems to have been created by Mylne from a pre-existing water feature dug in Elizabethan times by the Fermors' house chaplain, a Jesuit priest, and his assistant, who are credited with having spent more than twelve years digging it out.

The Temple of Peace on the northern edge of the lake at Tusmore, dedicated to Alexander Pope, was originally built by the Fermor family and has been carefully restored by the new owner, Mr Wafic Said.

At the back of the temple is a wooden board on which is a line written by Alexander Pope, possibly when he was staying at Tusmore. It reads: *'And Temples Rise The Beauteous Works of Peace.'*

The site of Tusmore's deserted medieval village situated in a field next to the cricket pavilion, five hundred yards north-west of Tusmore House. *The Victoria County History of Oxfordshire*, Vol. VI, records that the medieval village was one of the smallest and poorest in the Ploughley Hundred and was completely depopulated by the Black Death which arrived from India, via Weymouth, in 1348. Henry Rawlinson visited the site of Tusmore village in 1718 and recorded that the former medieval village church was then *'quite gone'* and no vestige remained. Aerial photographs and recent fieldwork suggest that the village consisted of at least five cottages in rectangular enclosures aligned on two hollow ways. Pottery finds also indicate that part of the medieval village was built on the site of a former Roman settlement.

Hardwick Church, situated about one mile south-east of Tusmore House in the hamlet of Hardwick, was almost entirely rebuilt in 1878 to the designs of G.G. Scott, junior. The stained glass in the west window by Burlison and Grylls was made to match the east window by Clayton and Bell. The church was often used as a place of worship by the Earls of Effingham and the cemetery contains several family graves.

The grave of the 4th Earl of Effingham at Hardwick. He was originally buried on the terrace at Tusmore House, but when the house was sold in 1928 the new owners had his body exhumed and reburied at Hardwick. Apart from having written several books on foreign travel, he was long remembered in the neighbourhood for annually distributing presents of toys to the local children at Christmas.

SHELSWELL PARK

Shelswell and its partner village Newton Purcell, which were officially united as a parish in 1932, have always been small. Traces visible near Home Farm probably mark the site of a moated medieval manor house and a deserted medieval village and the site of St Ebbe's church (which was disused from the 17th century and demolished by 1796) are found nearby. Richard Heath, the son of an Oxford brewer, who was holder of several civic offices, married the heiress to the manor, Dorothy Verney, and two statues in 16th century dress found at Newton Purcell and now displayed outside the church may represent this couple. The Trotman family built a new manor house on a different site in the early 18th century, which was largely rebuilt by Edward Slater Harrison to the design of William Wilkinson, in 1875. As the site is so close to Juniper Hill, the home of Flora Thompson, it is just possible that her father Albert Timms may have been employed there as a stonemason.

Edward's great-uncle, Gilbert Harrison, a London merchant, had purchased the manor in the late 18th century. Edward Slater Harrison is the inspiration for the *Sir Timothy* of Flora Thompson's *Lark Rise to Candleford*, but the suggestion in the television adaptation that he was romantically involved with the Fringford postmistress is spurious and not indicated in the book. However, he was the magistrate before whom Flora had to swear that she would not tamper with the mail when she first went to work for Mrs Whitton at the Post Office and it was while she was acting as letter carrier delivering the postbag to Shelswell that she met the young gamekeeper she christened *Philip White*.

Edward married Cecilia Selina Carhampton Saunderson in 1865. After her death in 1899 he married Emma Cecilia Cartwright, daughter of Richard Aubrey Cartwright, Deputy Lieutenant of Northamptonshire, in 1900. As gentry rather than aristocracy he kept a much smaller household than the Earl of Effingham: in 1881 he employed a butler, housekeeper, a German lady's maid, two housemaids, a kitchen maid, scullery maid, footman, and under-footman.

Edward Slater Harrison exerted much more influence on the local community than the Earl and when he died in April 1911 the *Bicester Advertiser* was lavish in its praise. As well as being a magistrate, during his long career he served as a Guardian of the Bicester Poor Law Union, a Rural District Councillor, Chairman of the Highways Board, a member of Oxfordshire County Council and Vice-President of the Bicester Branch of the YMCA.

He took his Oxfordshire Militia regiment to fight in the Crimean War and commanded the Bicester Troop of the Queen's Own Oxfordshire Hussars, retiring as Lieutenant-Colonel. He also supported the Bicester Hunt, exhibited at agricultural shows and was twice President of the Oxfordshire Agricultural Society and three times President of the Bicester Agricultural Association.

Edward Slater Harrison was described by the paper as *'one of the best'*, generous to his tenants and a benefactor to Newton Purcell and Hethe churches.

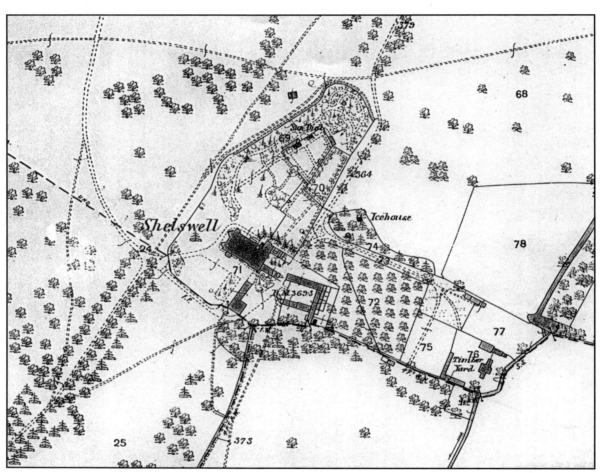

Ordnance Survey map of 1880 showing the location of the new Shelswell House built in 1875 by Edward Slater Harrison. Shortly before the Norman Conquest the manor of Shelswell was held by the Anglo-Saxon thegn, Edwin, son of Burred, and by the time of the compilation of the Domesday Book (1086), the manor had passed to Geoffrey, Bishop of Coutances. Following various changes of ownership the estate was purchased in the late 18th century by Gilbert Harrison, a London merchant, and it still remains with a branch of the Harrison family.

A group of people, possibly from Fringford and Hethe, believed to be on their way to Queen Victoria's Jubilee celebrations held in Shelswell Park.

The gamekeeper's house and lodge located on the Cottisford to Fringford road at a side entrance to the Shelswell estate.

SHELSWELL HOUSE, PULLED DOWN IN 1875.

Engraving showing the Shelswell House pulled down by Edward Slater Harrison in 1875. It was originally built by Sir John Cope around 1700 and enlarged by Fiennes Trotman (1743-1782).

Edward Slater Harrison of Shelswell Park, photographed with his dog Nell on 18 September 1902. Edward Slater Harrison was portrayed as the highly respected *Sir Timothy* in *Lark Rise to Candleford* and ran the estate from 1874 until his death in 1911. He had two wives, the first being Cecelia Selina Carhampton Saunderson, who died in 1899, and the second, Emma Cecelia Cartwright, who remained in possession of Shelswell until her death in 1943. Edward's first wife Cecelia was cast as the friendly *Lady Adelaide* by Flora Thompson in *Lark Rise to Candleford.* (Courtesy of Baroness Von Maltzahn)

Emma Cecelia Cartwright riding side-saddle on her horse *Surprise* shortly before her marriage to Edward Slater Harrison in 1900. Emma rode regularly with the Bicester and Warden Hill Hunt, of which she was a long-term member. (Photograph from the *Bicester and Warden Hill Hunt Book* compiled in 1898 by her friend Mrs Williamina Keith-Falconer of the Garth, Bicester)

William Wemyss Methven Dewar (1829-1903). William Dewar married Edward Slater Harrison's sister Augusta in 1857 and was buried in 1903 in Fringford church cemetery. For many years William and Augusta Dewar lived at Cotmore House, Fringford, which they built soon after their marriage. William W. M. Dewar was chairman of the Bicester Board of Guardians in the 1890s. His grandson, the kindly John Francis Dewar Harrison, succeeded to the Shelswell estate in 1943 and died in 1967.

JUNIPER HILL

Today Juniper Hill is best known as the village where Flora Thompson was born and which she immortalised as *Lark Rise* in her trilogy *Lark Rise to Candleford*, which evocatively described her rural childhood and the characters she knew in the late 19th century. However, Juniper has its own interesting story. It began life only in 1754 when the poor law overseers of Cottisford decided to raise a rate to build two houses for the poor in the middle of empty heathland at a cost of £28 7s 6d, about a mile and a half from the village. This was done because Cottisford was a 'closed' village under the control of Eton College, which did not want more development there and preferred to keep it for the local elite. It was called Juniper Hill because of the juniper bushes growing on the heath, the last of which can be seen in the former pub garden. Flora Thompson gave Juniper the name of *Lark Rise* because of the larks singing in the local fields and *The Rise* was the lane in which she lived.

Two more cottages were built soon afterwards and several more were built under squatters' rights, by which a person built a hearth and chimney and started a fire in it between dawn and dusk. Juniper became what was known as an 'open' village, which grew up higgledy-piggledy outside the control of a landowner, but this did not help the inhabitants when Cottisford parish, which included the village of Juniper, was enclosed in 1848. Many had a rude awakening on discovering that they did not own their houses after all and there was much unrest which led to the Juniper Hill riots, during which men tore down the notices about enclosure and attacked surveyors, which lasted until 1853. Several families were ejected from the village by the magistrates at Bicester Petty Sessions and others had to agree to pay rent on their cottages. In 1871 there were thirty-three cottages in the village.

Richard Moss, Flora's *Dick,* was one of the few who had a legal entitlement to his Juniper house, but several of his family were ejected and he only escaped by the skin of his teeth as he was a notorious poacher. Because Richard's family had owned the house before enclosure, when labourers were better off because they could more easily augment their incomes by grazing animals on waste ground and cutting wood and sedge, his was the best equipped in the village, according to Flora. He and his wife Sarah, née Stephens, (Flora's *Sally*) had a well-stocked garden and kept bees. Their house disappeared many years ago and Flora recalled that on one of her visits to Juniper as an adult all that was left of it was a mound in the field.

Nearly all the men in Juniper in 1871 were agricultural labourers, apart from Flora's father Albert Timms, a stonemason who worked in Brackley, Thomas Harris, the publican and grocer who ran the Fox Inn, and Thomas Whiting, Flora's uncle, who was a shoemaker. In the middle of the 19th century many women augmented their husbands' incomes by lacemaking and in Flora's time this tradition was carried on by her neighbour *Queenie Macey* (in real life Elizabeth Massey), although the industry had almost died out because of the advent of machine lace.

Albert and his wife Emma rented the End House, which Flora described as a double cottage. He was constantly dissatisfied, hoping to move somewhere better, but as his family grew there was less money and he was forced to stay put. He had ten children, four of whom died young. His eldest surviving daughter Flora (born in 1876), who married postmaster John Thompson, became a writer, which was most unusual as she came from a working-class background. Her writing is specially vivid and accurate because she actually experienced the rural life she wrote about. Flora's much-loved younger brother Edwin featured as *Edmund* in her books. He joined the army to fight in the Boer War in South Africa and later in India before emigrating to Canada. He returned to England as part of the Eastern Ontario Battalion to fight in the First World War. He was killed in action three weeks after arriving in France in 1916. May was born in 1884 and in 1901 was working in a Temperance Hotel in Dorking. Ethel Elizabeth, born in 1886, became a writer of children's books. Frank Wallington, born in 1888, later emigrated to Australia. The last surviving sibling was Annie Gertrude, born in 1900. Albert Timms died in 1918, aged 64, and is buried in Cottisford churchyard. Emma, his wife, died in 1933 and is buried in Hethe.

Cottisford did not boast a pub, so *The Fox* (Flora's *Waggon and Horses*) was the social centre for the local labourers, who came most evenings to talk politics and sing folk songs. In Flora's time the publican was widow Frances Harris, and in the 1890s Thomas Harris took over. He described himself as a pub-licensed victualler, as the pub had a small grocer's shop to provide for local needs. A baker and greengrocer and fish stall visited the village each week, but otherwise the nearest shops were three miles away in Brackley. Villagers either walked there or hitched a ride on the carrier's cart. When Flora commented on the changes which had taken place around the turn of the century, she commented wryly that the shop was selling tins of Australian rabbit!

Another important aspect of the village was the allotments, which gave the agricultural labourers a small measure of independence, as they grew potatoes and most of the other vegetables they needed, which helped to supplement their meagre incomes. Their wives grew herbs, some of which were used for medicinal purposes, in their gardens.

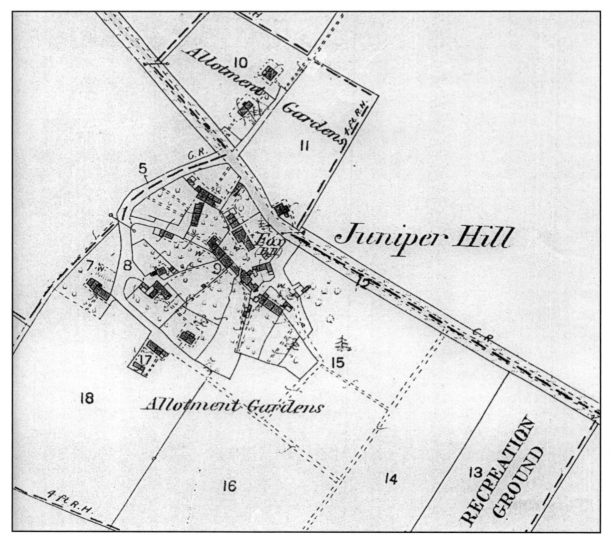

Ordnance Survey map showing the hamlet of Juniper in 1880. The settlement has changed little since the map was drawn up nearly one hundred and thirty years ago. Number 17 on the map marks the position of the End House where Flora Thompson lived as a child until 1891, after which time she went to live at the Forge and Post Office at Fringford.

The southern approach to Juniper from Cottisford in c1890 with *The Fox* public house acting as a landmark. Flora Thompson re-christened it the *Waggon and Horses* in *Lark Rise to Candleford*.

The frontage of *The Fox*, Juniper in the 1990s.

A shooting party with five gundogs outside *The Fox*, Juniper, in c1905. The man on the far left is the Earl of Effingham's gamekeeper Joseph Walby. The man fifth from the left, smoking a cigar, is the Earl of Effingham and the large man framed by the doorway is the licensee of the Fox, Anthony Wood.

A group of local men gathered outside the *Fox Inn*, Juniper, c1900-1905. It has been suggested that the man sitting immediately right of the doorway with a moustache may be Flora's brother Edwin Timms.

Schoolteacher David Morris and his wife Jean, the last licensee, standing outside *The Fox*, Juniper, before it closed in 1999.

The public bar of *The Fox*, Juniper, with John Watts sitting in the chair.

The *End House,* Juniper, where Flora Thompson lived with her parents and brothers and sisters between 1876 and 1891.

The *End House* photographed in 2007. The general proportions of the house appear to have changed little, although the positions of the back door and windows have altered.

Members of the Timms family in the garden of the *End House* in c1901. Mrs Violet McGovern, the niece of Flora Thompson, has identified those on the photo as follows: back row, left to right: Flora Thompson and her sister May; front row, left to right: unknown person and Flora's mother Emma Timms. The unknown person could be Flora's aunt, Ann Elizabeth Whiting, née Timms (1846-1932), the sister of her father Albert. Ann married shoemaker Thomas Whiting and lived most of her life in a cottage situated in School Lane at Twyford. (Courtesy of the Old Gaol Museum, Buckingham)

Flora's favourite younger brother, Edwin, photographed while he was serving in India in the Duke of Wellington's regiment, in c1903-1905. The medals he is wearing are probably those gained while serving with the regiment in the Boer War. Following his service in the Duke of Wellington's regiment, Edwin returned for a brief period to England, working as a farm labourer. Frustrated with his inability to better his position, he emigrated to Canada and following the outbreak of the First World War enlisted at Winnepeg on 12 December 1914 in the 32nd Overseas Infantry Battallion. After training, he was transferred into the Eastern Ontario Battalion and on 26 April 1916 was killed on the Western Front during a lull in the battle for the St Eloi crater. He was buried in grave 11 F3 in the Woods Cemetery at Zillebeke in Belgium. (Courtesy of Henry Westbury)

Queenie's Cottage, Juniper, as it appeared in the 1930s. The cottage lay alongside *The Rise*, and was situated in front of the *End House*. During Flora's childhood it was the home of Eliza Massey, née Gee, whom Flora cast as *Queenie*, the lacemaker and beekeeper in *Lark Rise to Candleford*. Eliza's husband Thomas died in the Bicester workhouse in 1899, and she herself died in 1902, aged 83. The 1901 census shows that Eliza was living with her daughter Annie in Albert Place, Crockwell, which was then one of the poorer parts of Bicester. (Courtesy of Banbury Museum)

Eliza Massey photographed in her Sunday best, with her hair carefully combed and parted and her coat tied up at the neck with a ribbon. She holds a small book in her hands, possibly a prayer book or bible.

COTTISFORD

The village of Cottisford, which Flora Thompson rechristened *Fordlow*, closely resembles the one she knew, as, apart from the level of the road rising, the school closing and the fact that some farm buildings have been converted to dwellings, the centre of the village is substantially the same as it was in the late 19th century.

Cottisford was the mother village of Juniper Hill. It existed before the Norman Conquest and control over it passed to the Norman Abbey of Bec in 1100. During the Hundred Years War French-controlled land was reclaimed by the Crown and in 1441 Henry VI granted it to his new foundation of Eton College, which exerted influence over the village for centuries. It was kept as a 'closed' village: the College restricted building, so that the main residents were the tenant of the Manor House, the principal farmers, the vicar (if he was resident), the schoolmistress and the blacksmith. The shepherd and superior farm labourers lived in the model cottages with their outside privies, wash-houses and pigsties built near the school in 1869 by the Earl of Effingham. The labourers who lived in cottages near the church, demolished in the early 19th century when William Turner enlarged Cottisford House, may have moved to cottages he built in their stead in the Warren north of the village, but they had disappeared by 1910. The peak population of Cottisford, including Juniper and the Warren, was 327 in 1871, dropping to 240 in 1881 and to 161 in 1901, reflecting the reduction in agricultural jobs with the advent of agricultural machinery, commented on by Flora.

The church, dedicated to St Mary, built in the 13th century, but much altered by Charles Buckeridge in 1860, has a particular charm. It contains a 16th century brass, probably of the Samwell family, who leased the manor, depicted with eight sons behind John Samwell, who died in 1505 (or possibly his son Robert who died in 1513) and five daughters behind his wife. Another memorial commemorates Richard Eyre, an employee of the East India Company for twenty-eight years who was a great benefactor to the village and died in 1761. Other memorials reflect some of the people whom Flora would have known, with the east and west windows decorated with diaphane work by the family of Squire Rousby, who lived at Cottisford House. One window was dedicated by Rector, Charles Sawkins Harrison (her *Mr Ellison*), the first for many years who actually lived locally in the rectory opposite the church, to his children George Sidney, who died in 1867, aged 8, and Amy Catherine, who died in 1868, aged 14. His wife Margaret died in her fifties, so it was her daughter Grace who took on the role of helping her father in the parish. She died a spinster in Oxford, aged 70. Her father went into the village school each day to teach the children religion, and, according to Flora, informed them that they had been born into a particular station in life and that was where they should stay. Despite his remoteness from the lowlier members of his congregation, he was a kindly man who had their best interests at heart and supported those in need.

Next to the church is Cottisford House, the site of a grange administered by the Prior of Ogbourne for the Abbey of Bec, which had a granary, fishponds and a dovecote. Eton College let the site and several different houses were built on it. The present house was built by Laurence Lord in the early 18th century, then doubled in size by William Turner, a member of the Irish bar, who took on the lease in 1825. He used the £20,000 dowry brought by his wife Maria Meares to improve the house and landscape his grounds, but he drastically overspent and fled to Belgium to avoid his creditors, dying in Bruges in 1836.

The Rousby family lived at Cottisford House from 1842 and Edwards Richard Kendall Rousby purchased it from Eton College in 1885. His mother Louisa would have been Flora's *Mrs Bracewell*, who often visited the school and helped the girls with their needlework. The family kept a small establishment: in 1881 Louisa was the head of the household as her son was at Oxford, and she had a resident butler cum gardener, cook, housemaid and servant and in 1891 she had a cook and two servants, with a groom/coachman living nearby. Flora described them as impoverished gentry.

Across the road, east of the Rectory is the Manor House, credited with being the oldest inhabited house in Oxfordshire. It was probably built in the 14th century by Sir Roger de Cotesford, incorporating parts of the earlier house including a window of c1200. In the 16th and 17th centuries it was enlarged and a floor was inserted above the hall and the roof rebuilt. Flora described it as a Tudor farmhouse and the strange little tower which she thought might have been a prison was probably built as a garderobe. The tenant in Flora's time was Joseph Waters. Flora commented on the field names, which reflect the history of the farm, Moat Close suggests that the medieval building was originally moated, Pond Piece Allotment indicated medieval fishponds, Dove House Piece the dovecote where doves were bred to be eaten on medieval 'fish days' and so on.

The school was built on a triangle at the crossroads in 1856 with a capacity of fifty children. The schoolmistress lived in a two-room cottage attached to it and there were earth closets in the yard. Flora's descriptions of her schooldays are vivid; it must have been hard for the teacher, with children varying in age from about four to fourteen. They were taught reading, writing and arithmetic, and in the afternoons the boys did drawing while the girls learnt needlework – the bane of Flora's life! It was important for them, as most of the girls would go into service and many would be required to use those skills, and they would often make and mend their own clothes. May Day formed the highlight of the school year: the children spent days making the garland, with the 'Lady', the doll in the centre, and they spent the whole day parading from house to house with the May King and Queen singing May songs.

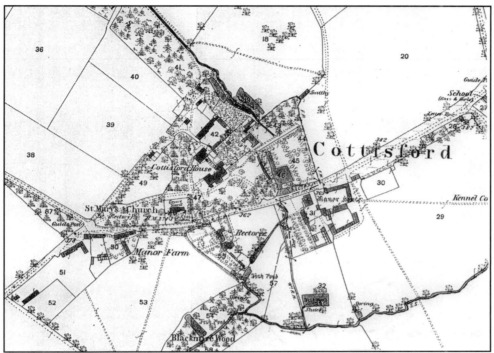

Ordnance Survey map surveyed in 1880 showing the centre of the old village of Cottisford. The main buildings were then and still are: the Church, Cottisford House, the Rectory, and the Manor House. The Victorian school attended by Flora Thompson and her younger brother Edwin lay outside the centre of the village near the junction of the Cottisford road with the roads to Juniper, Shelswell and Fringford.

St Mary's church, Cottisford, is small and consists of a nave, chancel and porch dating back to the 13th century. There is no tower and there was once a bellcote on the roof at the western end. (Courtesy of Martin Haslett)

The interior of the church looking east towards the chancel and stained glass in the east window dedicated to the memory of Edwards Edwards-Rousby, 1819-1875, who lived at Cottisford House. Flora Thompson portrayed the Rousbys as the *Bracewells* in *Lark Rise to Candleford*. (Courtesy of Martin Haslett)

14th century stone coffin in a recess near the east end of Cottisford Church thought to contain the remains of a member of the de Cotesford family. (Courtesy of Martin Haslett)

The brass probably made to commemorate the life of John Samwell, who died in 1505, showing him with his wife, eight sons and five daughters. (Courtesy of Martin Haslett)

The Revd Charles Sawkins Harrison, whom Flora Thompson immortalised as *Mr Ellison* in *Lark Rise to Candleford*. In real life his daughter Grace died a spinster in Oxford, aged seventy, but in the recent BBC television adaption she married *Thomas Brown* the postman, who worked in *Miss Lane's*, *Candleford* Post Office. (Courtesy of Cottisford and Hardwick Parochial Church Council)

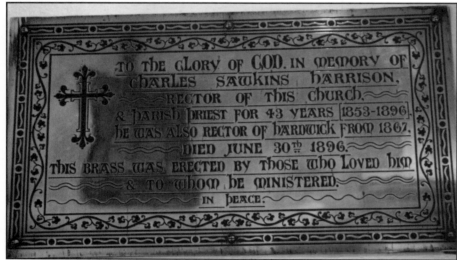

Wall tablet to the memory of the Revd Charles Sawkins Harrison, Rector of Cottisford, died 30 June 1896. (Courtesy of Martin Haslett)

The Rectory, the residence of Revd Charles Sawkins Harrison, Rector of Cottisford, 1853-1896, who restored the church and founded the school. He was portrayed by Flora Thompson as *Mr Ellison*, an old-fashioned and kindly autocrat.

Cottisford House lies next to the church in its own grounds and was built as a square-shaped hunting box with a hipped roof by Laurence Lord in c1700. In the 1870s the house was the home of the Rousby family. After the Second World War the property was the home of Sir Robert Brooke-Popham, who in 1940 had been appointed Commander-in-Chief of British Forces in the Far East. (Courtesy of Martin Haslett)

The funeral cortege of Sir Robert Brooke-Popham of Cottisford House passing through King's End, Bicester, on its way to the funeral service held on 23 October 1953, at St Edburg's church. The streets were lined with airmen for the occasion. He was later buried in Somerset. (Courtesy of William Harris Morgan)

Cottisford's medieval manor house, the earliest parts of which may have been constructed by the de Cotesford family. The tenant farmer in the time of Flora Thompson was Joseph Waters, who is mentioned in *Lark Rise to Candleford*.

The northern end of the manor house contains the tracery of several 15th century windows and the remains of a two-light attic window of c1200, which may have come from an earlier building. The gabled projection visible above the perimeter garden wall contained a garderobe, which opened off a solar. The octagonal chimney shaft seen above the projection is believed to be 14th century.

A blocked 15th century window in the north wall of the manor house. (Courtesy of Martin Haslett)

Kennel Cottages situated just outside Cottisford on the road to Fringford. The cottages may have accommodated staff attached to kennels which housed hounds belonging to Tusmore and Shelswell Park. A painting by Ben Marshall (1767-1835) shows Mr Fermor's hounds on Cottisford Heath, which could have been kept here.

HETHE

Hethe has several links with Flora Thompson, as Mary Whiting, the mother of *Uncle Tom*, was born here and Flora's mother Emma died here. It has also been suggested that Flora's novel *Still Glides the Stream* may have been partially based on Hethe.

The small parish, only about a mile long and half a mile wide, is situated on both sides of a stream, deriving its name from the Anglo-Saxon for 'uncultivated ground'. The church, dedicated to St Edmund, the Saxon King and martyr, was built on higher ground away from the original settlement in the 12th century, being rebuilt and enlarged in the late 13th and early 14th centuries, and the village expanded towards it. At the Norman Conquest it came into the possession of Geoffrey, Bishop of Coutances, and passed to Norman de Verdun who doubled the size of the Saxon settlement. A lesser manor passed into the hands of St Bartholomew's Hospital in Smithfield in the latter half of the 12th century.

The village was badly affected by the Black Death in 1349: it was said that 21 of the 27 villeins of the village were dead and their land was uncultivated, and in 1524 it had the third lowest taxable value of the villages in the Ploughley Hundred. The land called *The Flats* near the Cottisford border was used as a rabbit warren and in the 16th century tenants could kill rabbits near the brook to protect their corn. The village was enclosed in 1772, when the largest share of the land went to the Fiennes Trotman, the lord of the manor.

Agriculture was the most important economic influence on the village, but there were quite a few craftsmen and tradesmen: mason, carpenter, painter, builder and thatcher representing building trades, while a shoemaker, bootmaker and cordwainer, cooper and sawyer and five tailors and one tailoress and eight dressmakers served the needs of the village. A straw-hatmaker was mentioned in 1851. Other occupations included a lawyer, a magistrate, a policeman, errand boy, five laundresses, an innkeeper and a beer retailer, a butcher, grocer, baker and carrier.

The Rector in 1881 was Frederick Salter, aged 49, from Ottery in Devon. The school, which had opened in 1852, was run by the Church of England (the teacher in 1881 was Mary Cakebread, aged 34, from Sibford). The Catholic community from the villages around was served by the chapel of the Holy Trinity, which opened in 1832. The Harris family who ran the *Fox Inn* in Juniper Hill would have worshipped there. The Catholic school opened in 1870 to cater for fifty children, but the average attendance in 1889 was only eight, although seventy-seven village children were described as scholars in the 1881 census. Several village houses were licensed for Presbyterian worship and a Wesleyan chapel was built by 1854. The present one opened in 1876.

The Account Book of the *Hethe and Neighbouring Parishes Farmers' Association*, which represented the interests of local farmers, has survived for the years 1833-1881. It covered the area north of Bicester including Fringford, Cottisford, Tusmore, Stoke Lyne, Newton Purcell, Finmere, Mixbury, Stratton Audley, Goddington, Chetwode and Barton Hartshorn. Membership grew from five in 1833 to thirty in 1881. Membership was by invitation, and an annual subscription of five shillings was payable. The committee met monthly and the membership annually, often at the *Whitmore Arms* in Hethe (named after Thomas Whitmore who rented Hethe House and restored the inn), the *Butchers Arms* in Fringford or the *Crown Inn* in Sheep Street, Bicester. The Association acted as a body to call upon the parish constables, and, after 1857, the Oxfordshire constabulary, to deal with local crime affecting the members. For example James Goble, the Bicester parish constable, was called on to act in 1844:

In consequence of a man named Richard Gibbard [carpenter and wheelwright of Fringford] *having robbed Mr Mansfield* [possibly John Mansfield of Fringford] *of several articles and absconded, a meeting of the Committee of the Association was held at the Crown Inn Bicester, on 26 January 1844 for the purpose of considering what steps be taken in the matter, when it was resolved that Mr Goble the Constable of Bicester be requested to use his endeavours to apprehend him, and that an offer of three guineas from the association be made to Mr Goble on his conviction; Mr Mansfield at the same time offered two guineas for his apprehension.*

This was signed by farmers Thomas Simons of Fringford, William Mansfield of Stoke Lyne, William Crawford of Newton Purcell, Richard Harding of Finmere, John Roots of Goddington and G. Waten.

Mary Whiting, mother of Flora's *Uncle Tom*, was born in Hethe in 1819, the daughter of agricultural labourer Thomas Batchelor. She did not have an easy life as she married Austin Masters Whiting, a linen and woollen draper of Roade in Northamptonshire. Their children were John, born in 1845, Sarah, born in 1847 and Thomas, born in 1850. Austin's career declined and he became a hawker, then decided to emigrate to America, leaving his wife and family behind. Thomas was living with his grandparents Thomas and Harriet Batchelor in Cottisford in 1861 while his mother Mary was working as a housemaid in Hethe in the household of James Mitchell and his wife Jane. In 1871 he was living in Juniper Hill, working as a shoemaker, with his mother Mary (now described as a widow), who was working as a dressmaker. In 1881, aged 63, she was living alone in Hethe with no occupation, but by 1891 she must have run short of money as she was working as a general servant in Hethe. She appears to have lived with Thomas in old age as she died in Twyford in 1902 aged, 83.

Emma Timms, Flora's mother, moved to Hethe as a widow towards the end of her life, when she could no longer cope alone in the End House at Juniper Hill, to live with one of her daughters, and died and was buried there at the age of 80 in 1933.

Members of the Hethe branch of the Oddfellows Friendly Society crossing Hethe Bridge on Whit Monday in 1911. One of the main centres for the Oddfellows Society was at Brackley, for which records of members and the villages from which they came survive for the years 1845-1886. Flora Thompson's father, Albert Timms of Juniper Hill, is listed as a member in the subscription register. The brook in the foreground was known in the Middle Ages as the Wundred brook and may have inspired the title for Flora Thompson's book *Still Glides the Stream*, published by the Oxford University Press in 1948. The stream is a tributary of the river Ooze and is one of the largest flowing brooks in the area.

The watercress-filled Wundred brook looking north-west from Hethe bridge. The brook runs through a rich alluvial valley and it has been suggested that, when Norman de Verdun received a large land grant in Hethe in the middle of the 12th century, he deliberately settled a number of peasants along the stream in this area away from the existing Anglo-Saxon village near the parish church. Evidence for peasants being settled near the brook is attested by certain family names surviving in early medieval records, e.g. Roger by the Wundred Bridge, Henry atte Stream and Geoffrey by Wundred Brook. In the 16th century a large rabbit warren covering some eighty acres, was established west of the brook near the Cottisford boundary, beyond the hedge line which is visible on the horizon on the left.

Hethe Church, Bicester.

The parish church of Hethe dedicated to St Edmund and St George, built on an Oolitic lime-stone ridge in c1100. In 1859 the church was heavily restored and a north aisle constructed for the accommodation of the poor of the parish by the rector, the Revd Frederick Salter, according to plans drawn up by G. E. Street. Until the 1960s, the names of forty wage-earning householders in Hethe, who were deemed to rank as the longest residents in the village, were put up bi-annually on the church notice board. Each received four shillings in settlement of the village's ancient rights of common, lost when William Fermor of Tusmore enclosed the uncultivated ground of Hethe (the Heath of Hethe), which stretched from Hethe to Hardwick, by private act of Parliament in 1772. The act was passed on condition that William Fermor and his sucessors at Tusmore House paid £4 annually to the poor of Hethe to compensate them for their loss of common rights. It was decided to divide the £4 into forty equal portions.

The interior of Hethe church looking east towards the chancel. On the right can be seen the rectangular 'Lepers' squint in the south aisle, through which those with infectious diseases could view services in isolation. A complete list of rectors serving at Hethe exists back to the year 1232. One of the most distinguished rectors was Master Adam de Senestan (resident 1233-1268), who studied and lectured at Paris University and was a truly exceptional scholar. When he died at Hethe, he bequeathed his very valuable collection of books to Oseney Abbey, Oxford, where he was buried.

The Roman Catholic church dedicated to the Holy Trinity situated on the outskirts of Hethe was built in 1831 at a cost of £800 on a piece of land secured the year previously by Alfred Mcquire. The church served a substantial local Catholic community, numbering over 350 when the church first opened. Prior to the building of the church, Catholics held services in local houses, a favourite place of worship being the long gallery at the top of Hardwick Manor House. In the 17th century the Fermor family of Tusmore House maintained its own Catholic priest, who in times of danger was concealed in a priest hole, entered via a trap door hidden under a window seat. (Courtesy of Martin Haslett)

A shrine dedicated to the Virgin Mary under a yew tree at the Roman Catholic church.

The following letter dated 21 November 1912, was sent by L.M. Birch, the head teacher at St Philip's Roman Catholic School at Hethe, to Dr Cecil Morgan Hendriks at Bicester. It reads:

Dr Hendriks

Dear Sir,

Will you please make it convenient to call upon me at some time tomorrow Friday as I have had a very disagreeable encounter regarding one of the children named Lester. I sent her home on Wednesday afternoon as she had some spots on her face. – you came yourself and told me to send the scholars home as soon as I noticed this. I did so. Now the child is brought up here as having nothing at all the matter with it. I am dictated to and ordered about by Mr Lester (P.C.) as to what my duties are and what your duties are and I am further ordered to report the case to you whether it is Chicken Pox or not. This will not be necessary if you will please come here and see me so that I can better explain matters. I do not feel satisfied until I see you as then you can judge how things stand. I hope to see you tomorrow Friday and remain yours truly,

L.M.Birch (Head Teacher)

In this photograph a family group, possibly returned from a funeral (some are dressed in black), stand behind three wooden beehives in front of a cottage near the school in the Hardwick Road, Hethe. Both this cottage and its neighbour (known as Bateman's) have been demolished. The photograph calls to mind the custom of *telling the bees* the news of a bereavement that Flora Thompson recorded in *Lark Rise to Candleford*.

Hethe House, situated opposite the parish church, was built in the 18th century as a Dower House by the Trotman family of Shelswell Park. From 1911 to 1913 it was the temporary home of Major Arthur William Dewar-Harrison, who succeeded Edward Slater Harrison as owner of Shelswell Park, but could not live in the park as Edward's widow, Emma Cecelia, continued to live there until her death in 1943.

The Whitmore Arms has been the village public house since the 18th century, when it was called the *Maltsters Arms*. In 1808 the building was restored by Shropshire gentleman, Thomas Whitmore, who renamed the inn after himself. From c1831 to 1881 *The Whitmore Arms* was the favourite venue for the monthly meetings of *The Hethe and Neighbouring Parishes Farmers Association,* which met to protect the interests of local farmers against crime, particularly rick-burning. By 1881 (when the records cease) the *Hethe Association* had thirty members drawn from the area three to eight miles north of Bicester. The annual subscription for membership was five shillings.

Farm labourers drinking cider from stoneware jars while taking a break from making sheaves on *Wyatt's Farm*, Hethe, in about 1890. The three horses on the left had been used to tow a 'Sailor', which was a converted mowing machine fitted with three sails, of which only one is visible here. 'Sailors', produced sheaves of corn, which were thrown out to one side and then tied by hand by the labourers. They were widely used on farms in north-east Oxfordshire and in the Aylesbury Vale until the 1930s. This photograph, taken by Arthur James of Bicester, belonged to Mrs Whitton at Fringford, and hung on the wall of the Post Office when Flora Thompson lived there. (Courtesy of William Plumb)

FRINGFORD

In the hamlet there lived only one class of people; all did similar work, all were poor and all equal. The population of Candleford Green was more varied. It had a clergyman of its own and doctor and independent gentlewomen who lived in superior cottages with stabling attached, and artisans and labourers who lived in smaller and poorer ones ... Then there were shopkeepers and the schoolmaster and a master builder... the village was a little world in itself ... In the large country houses around lived squires and baronets and lords who employed armies of indoor servants, gardeners and estate workers. The village was their village, too: they attended its church, patronised its shops, and had influence on its affairs.

Flora Thompson, *Lark Rise to Candleford*

The village of Fringford must have seemed very cosmopolitan to Flora Thompson when she arrived here in 1891 to begin work, at the age of fourteen, in the Post Office attached to the smithy, both run by the formidable character Kezia Whitton. Although Fringford was the actual village where she worked, Flora admitted that *Candleford Green*, although containing elements of Fringford, is an amalgamation of several places, and some characters (such as the doctor) and institutions relate more to Bicester.

The area has been inhabited for over two thousand years and there was a Roman villa at Fringford Lodge. The place name, 'ford of Fera's people', suggests an early date for the two Anglo-Saxon settlements. After the Norman Conquest the land formed part of vast estates granted to Odo, William I's powerful half-brother, who granted it to Wadard, one of the few men mentioned by name on the Bayeux Tapestry. It passed to the Arsic family and the de Greys, and by the late 15th century was held by the Lovell family of Minster Lovell. Sir Thomas More held the manor in the 16th century and then after his death it went to Henry Norreys, who was charged with adultery with Anne Boleyn and executed. Only a few fragments of the medieval village remain, such as the Norman and Decorated arcades in the church (which was largely rebuilt in the 19th century) and the fifteenth century font and rood screen.

The 1662 hearth tax listed 35 houses but the village was in decline as in 1665 there were only 24. There was no large manor house and the main buildings were the Rectory and four large farm houses, two belonging to the Addington family. The village became more prosperous from the 18th century onwards and the number of houses increased from 42 in 1768 to 80 in 1851 and 94 in 1901 and the population increased from 252 in 1801 to 479 in 1871.

The land was enclosed in 1762 and in the early 19th century Arthur Young commented that the crops of barley, clover, wheat and oats suited the stonebrash soil. The Post Office and Smithy formed the heart of the village, a fact relished by Kezia Whitton. Her character inspired Flora Thompson's *Miss Lane*, the postmistress, but the physical description differed considerably as Mrs Whitton, far from being the *'little birdlike woman'* described in *Lark Rise to Candleford*, weighed about 18 stone and when she died in 1898 an upstairs window had to be taken out so that her coffin could be lowered out through it, as it was too large to get down the stairs.

She was born in 1835, the daughter of Alexander Kirby, a blacksmith from Stoke Lyne. She and her husband, John Whitton (the son of a saddler, who was born in Weston, Northamptonshire in 1830), were, installed at the forge in Fringford in 1854 when John was only twenty-four. In 1871 they had one apprentice blacksmith living with them, and in 1881 they also had a living-in servant, Zilpha Hinks (who later became a letter carrier). By 1891 there were two blacksmiths, one of them, Frederick William Plumb, living in the house and their servant was Winifred Waring. John died in 1891 and at a time when most widows would have retired, Kezia took on the running of the forge and wheelwright's shop as well as the Post Office. Her right-hand man was Frederick William Plumb from Fritwell, who leased the forge for twenty years after Mrs Whitton's death. As well as shoeing horses at the forge, the blacksmiths took a portable forge to local hunting stables, repaired agricultural machinery and made carts, putting the iron tyres on the wheels.

The Post Office was situated in the cross passage of the house. Flora sorted the morning mail, which arrived from Bicester at 7 a.m., in the wash-house, and as well as working behind the counter, she was a letter carrier, which gave her a chance to walk in the countryside and learn more about natural history. She delighted in Mrs Whitton's books, which she read voraciously. There were a few problems fitting in with her new regime – Mrs Whitton only had her washing done every six weeks, so Flora, who did not have enough clothes to survive that long, sent her dirty washing home every week to her mother on the carrier's cart.

Mrs Whitton was proud of her antique furniture, inherited from her family, and vividly described by Flora Thompson, including the oak dresser with its willow-pattern plates and the grandfather clock. An inventory made after her death listed four bedrooms with bedsteads, coloured quilts, Windsor chairs, tapestry carpets and mahogany furniture.

After Mrs Whitton's death the Post Office moved to the other side of the village. However, although now a private house, the post office and forge building is easily identifiable on the right side of the main road leading to the church and Manor Farm.

Fringford boasted several shops, including a butcher, baker and grocer, and Flora's description of *Tarmans* the grocers is based on that of the Mansfields, which opened in the 1860s as a butcher and grocer. However, her dress shop, run by *Ruby* and *Pearl* must have been transposed from elsewhere.

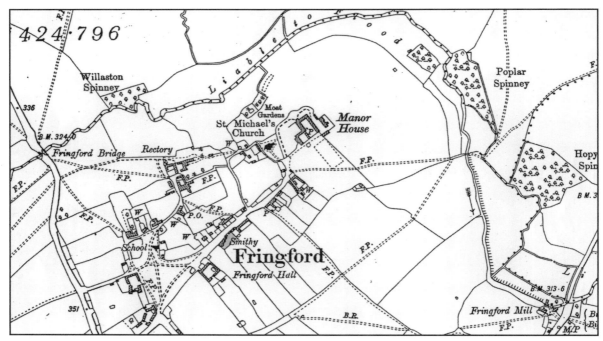

Ordnance Survey map showing Fringford in c1900. Flora Thompson lived with Mrs Whitton and her household in the building marked *Smithy* from 1891 to 1895. Following the death of Mrs Whitton's husband John Whitton in 1891, the smithy was run by her foreman, Frederick William Plumb. It was one of three blacksmith's shops operating in the village until the 1930s.

Rectory Lane looking north near Fringford church on a summer's day in the 1930s.

Pupils of Fringford School photographed outside the old school-house opposite the school in 1910/1911, including Billy Daniels (front row, fourth from right), Emily Plumb, born 1903 (front row, third from right), William Plumb, 1902-1973 (back row, third from left), Cecil Cross, later butcher of Fringford with shop opposite the Forge (back row, eighth from left) and Agnes Plumb, 1901-2001, back row, far right. (Courtesy of William Plumb)

Fringford ladies' cricket team photographed with the Bicester men's team at Fringford in 1915. Agnes Plumb of the Forge sits in front and is marked with a cross. (Courtesy of William Plumb)

The Forge and Post Office at Fringford in the 1880s. John Whitton, the postmaster and blacksmith, stands in front of a spring cart, while his wife Kezia (Flora Thompson's *Miss Lane*) holds the horse's head. Zilpha Hinks the family servant stands in the doorway. The little girl has yet to be identified. The three men on the left are, left to right: William Elderfield (carrying a sledge-hammer), unknown, and Frederick William Plumb. The metalled area in the grass in the foreground was used as a tyring platform for placing metal tyres round the wooden cart-wheels. This photograph is one of three which are known to have hung in the Post Office during the time that Flora Thompson was resident. (Courtesy of William Plumb)

A closer view of the Forge at Fringford in c1895 with Frederick William Plumb sitting in the cart on the left. The two boys may be Mrs Whitton's grandsons Arthur and Cuthbert and one of the blacksmiths could be Thomas Hicks, who was resident in the house when the census was taken in 1901. The deeds of the Forge date back to 1719 and quote the existence of earlier deeds which suggest that the building may have been constructed in c1597. Several deeds contain a clause asserting the right to stand ladders on the adjacent former Addington property to carry out thatching and other repairs on the west end of the building. (Courtesy of William Plumb)

Fringford postmaster and blacksmith, John Whitton (1830 –1891), and his wife Kezia, née Kirby, flanked, left, by their son Alexander Kirby Whitton (1866-1889), local auditor of the Gold Coast Company, and, right, by their son George Whitton (born 1863), a customs and excise officer in Liverpool. Behind the Whitton family stands the family's blacksmith foreman, Frederick William Plumb (1859-1930). The photograph may have been taken at Hethe and dates from c1888. (Courtesy of William Plumb)

Previously unpublished photograph of postmistress Mrs Kezia Whitton in her latter years photographed at the Fringford Post Office in about 1898. (Courtesy of William Plumb)

Mrs Whitton photographed with her foreman Frederick William Plumb in the late 1890s. (Courtesy of William Plumb)

Gravestones erected to the memory of Kezia and John Whitton behind the church in Fringford churchyard. The two gravestones are accompanied by a third in memory of their son, Alexander Kirby Whitton, who died of fever in 1889 and was buried at Accra on the African Gold Coast.

Frederick William Plumb in the 1880s. He was born in Fritwell and came to serve a seven-year apprenticeship with John Whitton when he was sixteen. Flora Thompson portrayed him as *Matthew*, *Miss Lane's* trusted foreman of the smithy in *Lark Rise to Candleford*. Flora described *Matthew* as being highly skilled in his ability to treat sick horses. She also recorded details of his veterinary cabinet, which still survives. Frederick William Plumb died in 1930 and is buried near the entrance to Fringford Cemetery not far from William Wemyss Methven Dewar, chairman of the Bicester Board of Guardians, who also features in *Lark Rise to Candleford*. (Courtesy of William Plumb)

The children of Frederick William Plumb standing outside the front door of the former Fringford Post Office in about 1910. They are, left to right: Agnes Elizabeth Plumb (1901-2001), a teacher of the blind in London, William Plumb (1902-1973), a garage mechanic, who worked for George Layton at his garage in London Road, Bicester, and Emily Leah Plumb (1903-c1980), a teacher in Surrey. All three children were born at the forge. (Courtesy of William Plumb)

William Plumb, the only son of Frederick William Plumb, holding the bellows handle in Fringford forge in c1940.

A family gathering of the Plumb family with relatives in the front room of Mrs Whitton's former Post Office in 1978. Sitting, left to right, are: Mrs Edith Plumb (1904-1999), the daughter-in-law of Frederick William Plumb, Edith Plumb's mother Mrs Beatrice Richardson of Stratton Audley (1883-1978), and Edith Plumb's sister Mrs Dorothy Ayris of Bicester (1903-1992). Behind them stands Mrs Molly Watts, née Waine, a cousin of Flora Thompson, and Mrs Beryl Plumb, daughter- in- law of Edith Plumb. After Mrs Whitton's death in 1898, Frederick Plumb rented the property from the Whitton family and purchased it in 1923 with a mortgage secured from the *Oddfellows Friendly Society*. Four generations of the Plumb family lived there from 1875 to 1994.

The L-shaped house of the Addington family situated next to the Forge and Post Office. The three-storey property, known as Hall Farm, the largest house in the village, was the property of the Addington, family from c1600 to the 1950s. The most illustrious member was Henry Addington, born 1757, who was elected Speaker of the House of Commons in 1796 and served as Prime Minister to George III from 1801 to 1804. He was created Viscount Sidmouth in January 1805.

In the 1880s James Blomfield related two stories told by the then Lord Sidmouth. The first was that a member of the Addington family rode regularly around the extensive cellars on a white horse after getting drunk on the large quantities of beer stored within. The second was that a family member sold a farm at Bainton (two miles from Fringford) for 2000 guineas and then rode safely back to the house with the money stored in his saddlebags. This was regarded as a considerable feat in those days.

Exterior of Fringford church in 1905. The church was largely rebuilt in the middle of the 19th century under the guidance of the Oxford Diocesan Architect G. E. Street.

A 13th century capital in Fringford church carved with medieval ladies wearing wimples. The noses of the faces were possibly deliberately damaged at the time of the Reformation.

Capital with medieval male faces, opposite the capital carved with the ladies. (Courtesy of Martin Haslett)

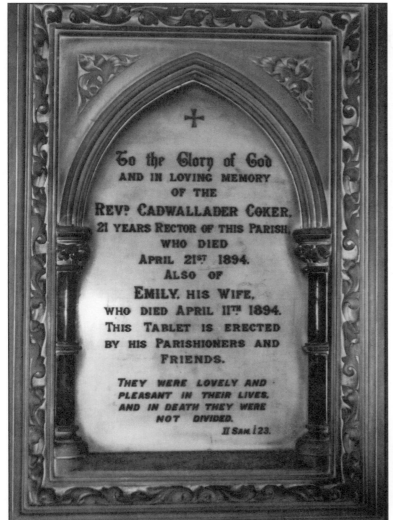

Wall tablet in the chancel dedicated to the memory of the Revd Cadwallader Coker and his wife Emily, who died suddenly in April 1894 within a few days of each other. Cadwallader Coker, who came from Bicester and served as Rector of Fringford in the 1890s, was portrayed by Flora as the amiable *Mr Coulsdon* in *Lark Rise to Candleford*. (Courtesy of Martin Haslett)

The tombstone of William Wemyss Methven Dewar of Cotmore House, who died in 1903. The tombstone is situated near the entrance to the churchyard.

STRATTON AUDLEY

Stratton Audley is named after the Audley family, who acquired the manor through James Audley, who married Ella, daughter of heiress Idonea de Camville and William Longespée. The Audleys built a castle, long destroyed, on the site of the present Court Close. Until the 19th century Stratton was in the unenviable position of being partly in Buckinghamshire and partly in Oxfordshire.

The most illustrious member of the family was Sir James Audley, a founder member of the Order of the Garter, who had a stall in St George's Chapel, Windsor. At the battle of Poitiers in 1356 he positioned himself and his four esquires at the front of the English army and attacked Arnold d'Audreghen, the Marshal of France, severely wounding him and routing his entourage. He fought valiantly all day and was carried off the field covered in blood and severely wounded. On the orders of the Black Prince he was brought to the royal tent to receive the accolade of being the bravest knight on the field and was rewarded with an annuity of 500 marks. He distributed the first instalment among his four esquires and, when the Prince heard of his generosity, he awarded him 600 more marks. Sir James fought in France and Spain and became governor of Aquitaine in 1367 and seneschal of Poitou in 1369.

Gilbert Basset, grandson of the Gilbert Basset who was lord of the manor at Stratton from 1086, founded Bicester Priory and endowed it with an estate at Stratton which passed at the Dissolution of the Monasteries to Christ Church, Oxford. The priory was jealous of its rights: in 1423, in very bad weather, two people were buried in the chapel at Stratton Audley, which infringed the priory's privileges, so the prior brought an expensive court case against the parishioners. Proceedings were heard in Stratton Audley church before the Bishop of Winchester, who listened to the *evidence of old men in divers towns* as to whether *at any time in their days they saw, or in the days of their fathers, heard of any burials being made there.* Judgement was that the bodies should be exhumed and reburied in Bicester churchyard. In 1455 the parish secured parochial independence of Bicester but Bicester Priory agreed to pay to keep a chaplain at Stratton to administer the sacrament. In 1520 it was recorded that services were not being held at regular hours and that the officiating canon had had to be removed because of *ill conduct with women.*

During the Civil War Mainwaring's Red Regiment was quartered at Stratton in 1643. A year later King Charles's forces stayed there and a skirmish took place nearby in 1645 at which the defeated Parliamentarian Captain Abercromby was fatally wounded. A circular earthwork known as Stuttle's Bank may be of Civil War date.

In the 19th century lacemaking was the chief occupation of the local women with twenty seven lacemakers recorded in 1851. A major occupation among the men, apart from agriculture, was stone quarrying. The quarries are rich in fossils in the Jurassic white limestone, forest marble and cornbrash rocks. The village also contains ancient woodland.

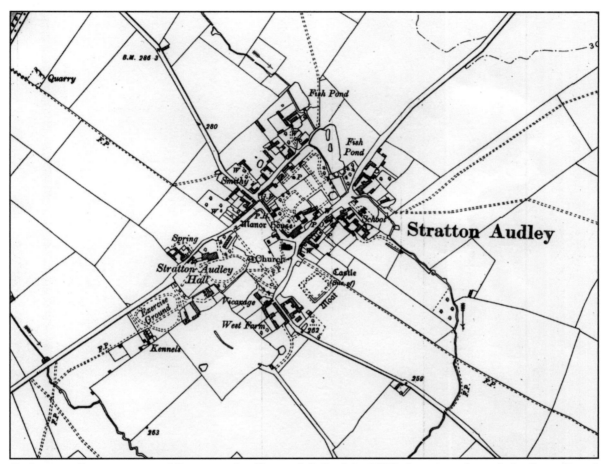

Ordnance Survey map of Stratton Audley published in 1900 showing the original medieval street plan, which takes the form of a letter H. Excluding the church, whose existing structure dates back to the 12th century, the oldest surviving domestic building is the manor house, which lies directly opposite. The western corner of the building is known as the 'Court House' and was probably built by John Borlase in 1545.

STRATTON AUDLEY

The parish church of St Mary and St Edburg, constructed from the 12th to the 15th centuries. For many years the church was under the control of Bicester Priory and until 1455 parishioners needing marriages and burials had to go to Bicester for the '*priviledge*'. There, they are known from surviving accounts to have made gifts to the church of up to 18d for a marriage and up to 15d for a burial. Due to inclement weather two Stratton parishioners were buried at Stratton Audley in 1423 and, fearing loss of income, the prior of Bicester brought and won a law suit against the village.

The site of the moated medieval castle of the Audley family, who held the larger of the two manors of Stratton Audley in the 13th and 14th centuries. Little is known of the castle except that it was roughly square in plan and was encompassed by a moat, part of which survives in a field south-east of the parish church. In 1263 Henry III granted a tree from his forest at Brill to repair the castle and substantial stone foundations were unearthed in the mid 19th century. The Audleys came into possession of Stratton Audley when William Longespée's daughter Ella married James Audley in 1244. In 1273 she settled the manor on her fifth and youngest son Hugh, who took part in the French and Scottish wars and was summoned to Parliament in 1321. He later joined Thomas of Lancaster's rebellion against Edward II and died a prisoner in Wallingford Castle in 1326.

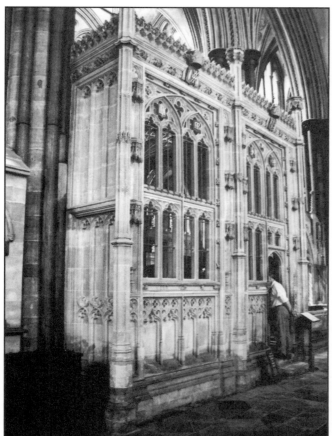

Chantry chapel in Salisbury Cathedral built by Edmund Audley, who was buried here in 1524. Edmund was made Bishop of Salisbury in 1502 and served as the executor to King Henry VII's will in 1509.

Mill Street looking north, with the farmhouse of Elm Farm visible in the distance. On the left is the 19th century gabled front of Sir John Borlase's 16th century manor house. The Borlase family succeeded to the medieval manor of the Audleys and probably used the remains of their nearby medieval castle to provide building stone for the manor house. (Courtesy of Martin Haslett)

Stratton Audley, Bicester.

Monument in the parish church erected in a grand baroque style to the lord of the manor, Sir John Borlase, who died 1689, with a reclining figure of Sir John dressed in Roman armour and a periwig, flanked by two weeping figures and framed by two large twisted columns. (Courtesy of Martin Haslett)

The fish pond at the north end of Cherry Street. The pond was considerably enlarged in the 18th century when a member of the Borlase family undertook unsuccessful 'mining' operations in a search for coal. In c1910 it was the home of a solitary swan which was well-known in Stratton Audley for tapping its beak on the front door of the thatched cottage on the right to be fed by Mrs Beatrice Richardson.

Thatched cottages in the Bicester Road looking north-east in 1905. The cottage at the top facing down the road has now gone. Some of the cottages housed staff who worked at Stratton Audley Hall, which is situated in its own grounds a short distance away. The Hall became the base for the Bicester Hunt when Thomas Tyrwhitt-Drake moved here in the middle of the 19th century and built the kennels. He was Master of the Hunt from 1851 to 1866 and was succeeded by Viscount Valentia and then Lord Chesham, who both rented Stratton Audley Hall. The Hall remains the centre for the Bicester and Warden Hill Hunt and provides stabling for horses and the Bicester hounds.

Wall tablet in the church commemorating the life of Charles Compton William Cavendish, 3rd Baron Chesham, who was killed from a fall while hunting near Daventry on 9 November 1907. He was Master of the Bicester and Warden Hill Hunt from 1884 to 1893. (Courtesy of Martin Haslett)

Portrait of Charles Compton William Cavendish, 3rd Baron Chesham (1850-1907), who
died from a fall while hunting.

Colonel George Gosling of Stratton Audley
Park, photographed for the Bicester and
Warden Hill Hunt book in 1898.

The large Victorian mansion house of Stratton Audley Park, situated in open country one
mile north of the village near the Roman road which forms the parish boundary with Fringford and Caversfield. It was built as a hunting box for the banking family of Glen in 1860
and was purchased by Colonel George Gosling in 1889. The Gosling family were keen sup-
porters of the Bicester and Warden Hill Hunt and remained in occupation until recent times.

The substantial stables of Stratton Audley Park built around a courtyard containing a dog pound in the c1920s. (Courtesy of Martin Haslett)

The Prince of Wales, later King Edward VIII, leaving Bicester North railway station en route to Stratton Audley to ride out with the Bicester and Warden Hill Hunt in 1928. The man doffing his hat is local newspaper reporter 'Tessie' Clifton. (Courtesy of William Harris Morgan)

The Goss family photographed in c1938. The family lived at Elm Farm and from the 1940s to the 1960s operated the Stratton Audley stone quarry near RAF Bicester. Left to right, are brothers George, Eric, Norman and Arthur, with their parents Edward and 'Lou'. Norman was killed in the Second World War, aged 22, and is commemorated by a wall tablet in Stratton Audley church. (Courtesy of William Harris Morgan)

Farmer Arthur Goss with his son Christopher and their two pigs, which had just taken the special prize at the 1964 Bicester Prime Stock Show held at Christmas. Local butcher Ted Goble of 50 Sheep Street, Bicester, stands in a white smock in the background. (Courtesy of Michael Morgan)

The vertebra of a Brontosaurus recovered from Stratton Audley stone quarry in 1940. The remains of three dinosaurs were found in the quarry during the Second World War. Building stone has been quarried commercially on a large scale in the parish since the 13th century. (Courtesy of Martin Haslett)

CHETWODE

The name Chetwode probably derives from the Saxon word 'chit', meaning cottage, and the parish is situated in the old forest of Rockwood. The Chetwode family held the manor from the late 12th century until 1966. Manorial courts were still being held in the mid 19th century, as this notice testifies:

> *The Manor of Chetwode in the County of Buckingham.*
> *Notice is hereby given, that a General Customary Court, with the View of Frankpledge, with the Court Baron of Sir John Newdegate Ludford Chetwode, Baronet, Lord of the said manor, will be holden at the Plough Inn, in Chetwode aforesaid, within the said Manor, on ... the ... day of ... next, at the Hour of Eleven o'Clock in the Forenoon precisely, when and where all Resiants and Customary Tenants of the said Manor are required personally to be and appear and do and perform their Suit and Service, and to pay their Rents, as of right they ought to perform and render at such Courts respectively.*
> *Dated this ... day of ... one thousand eight hundred and fifty-...*
>
> *Steward*

In 1245 Ralf de Norwich, who owned land in Chetwode, founded a small priory for three or four canons on land given by Henry III. He reserved the right to a house for his lifetime, for which he paid the prior two pounds of wax annually. In 1290 the prior and canons were granted the right to hold an annual three-day fair on the feast of the Nativity of the Blessed Mary. The priory came under the control of Notley Abbey and after dissolution in 1540 the site of the priory was granted to William Risley, whose family held it until the 19th century, although it sometimes descended down the female line.

In the late 12th or early 13th century Robert de Chetwode founded a hermitage dedicated to St Stephen and St Lawrence, which may have been situated south of the priory on a moated site. The last reference to a person living there was John Cowpere in 1359.

The village had its own church, dedicated to St Martin, which was acquired by the Priory of Chetwode around 1389 and surrendered to Notley Abbey in 1460. As the church was in a state of decay by 1480, the priory church became the main parish church except for fourteen days a year when services were to be held in St Martin's church. The Abbot of Notley was permitted to take materials from St Martin's church so long as the east end was enclosed, and the lord of the manor was to maintain it. This led to disputes and in the 16th century the Risleys, who owned the manor, were accused of taking materials, including the bells, driving out parishioners listening to divine service, erecting a well and a lime house in the church and putting cattle in the churchyard.

In 1460 the quire and north chapel of the priory church became the parish church. The nave and other priory buildings disappeared, although there are visible traces of moats and fishponds.

The Chetwode family have an ancient rite, said, like the Horn Tenure at Boarstall, to have been granted because a 'Lord of Chetwode' killed an enormous wild boar which was terrorising the area, as related in rhyme:

> *Then he blowed a blast full north, south, east, and west –*
> *Wind well thy horn, good hunter;*
> *And the wild-boar then heard him full in his den,*
> *As he was a jovial hunter.*
>
> *Then he made the best of his speed unto him –*
> *Wind well thy horn, good hunter;*
> *Swift flew the boar, with his tusks smeared with gore,*
> *To Sir Ryalas, the jovial hunter.*
>
> *Then the wild-boar, being so stout and so strong –*
> *Wind well thy horn, good hunter;*
> *Thrashed down the trees as he ramped him along,*
> *To Sir Ryalas, the jovial hunter.*
>
> *Then Sir Ryalas he drawed his broad sword with might –*
> *Wind well thy horn, good hunter;*
> *And he fairly cut the boar's head off quite,*
> *For he was a jovial hunter.*

The Chetwode family were granted the right, possibly around 1283, to take the Rhyne Toll on all cattle found on common land known as the Rhyne within the liberty of Chetwode from about 29 October for nine days. The area covered portions of Barton Hartshorn, Bourton, Cowley, Gawcott, Hillesden, Lenborough, Prebend End, Preston Bissett and Tingewick. This was valuable, as drove roads passed through, taking cattle from Wales and Ireland to London. *Records of Buckinghamshire* (Vol. III, 1863) records that the Rhyne at that time started at 9 o'clock on 30 October, when a horn (or a whelk shell) was blown at Church Hill in Buckingham and gingerbread and beer were distributed to assembled boys (girls were not permitted to partake). The bearer of the cakes and ale proceeded through Tingewick and blew the horn again at the Red Lion at Finmere, and again distributed refreshments to the boys, then the Rhyne began. Toll collectors stationed in Buckingham and Gawcott levied a toll at two shillings a score on all cattle and swine driven through the townships mentioned above until 7th November. Farmers and local landowners avoided paying the toll by giving the Chetwodes a shilling each per year. Those refusing to pay could be taken to court or have their animals impounded.

Earlier the Rhyne had started at daybreak and the toll demanded was two pence for the mouth and one penny per foot for each animal. After the opening of the railways, animals were transported by train instead of on foot so the value of the toll greatly decreased and was rented out at twenty-five shillings per year in 1863, whereas £20 or more had been raised at the beginning of the 19th century. The toll was last taken in 1889.

In 1810 a local farmer levelled a mound surrounded by a ditch, known as Boar's Pond, and discovered bones thought at the time to be those of the giant boar, but they have since been identified as belonging to a mammoth and wild horse.

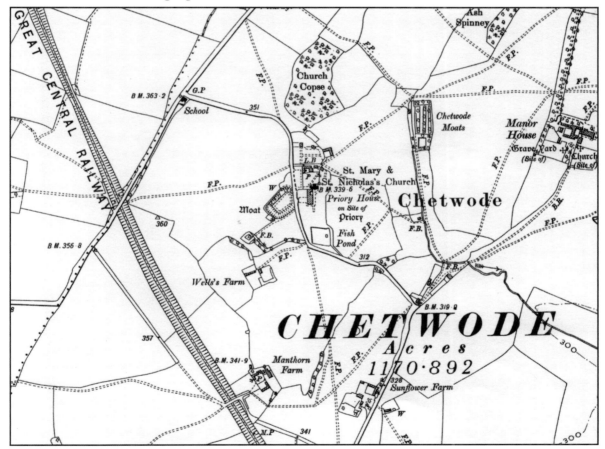

Ordnance Survey map showing the scatter of isolated farms constituting Chetwode in 1900. Chetwode was never a nucleated village, although the remains of a former Augustinian Priory lay at the centre of the 1171 acre parish. It is first mentioned in an Anglo-Saxon charter dating from 949, when Aelfstan sold Aethelflede 20 'manentes' at Chetwode and Hillesden.

Chetwode Church.

The church of St Mary and St Nicholas is almost all that remains of the medieval priory of Augustinian canons founded by Ralf de Norwich in about 1245. The priory was never wealthy and was dissolved in 1460. By 1480 the former priory church had fallen into disrepair and was handed over to the parishioners, who demolished the nave and utilised the former choir and chancel as their parish church.

The tower seen here was erected in 1480 and contains a bell dating from 1350, which carries the inscription *'John Chetwode who loved thee for ever O' Christ, gave me to thee.'*

Priory House, built on the site of the cloister, seen with the church of St Mary and St Nicholas in the background.

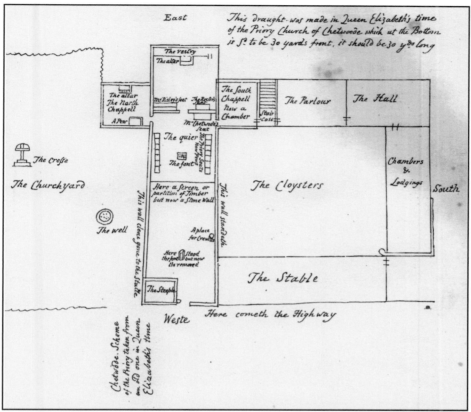

East

This draught was made in Queen Elizabeth's time of the Priory Church of Chetwoode which at the Bottom is s.d to be 30 yards front, it should be 30 y.ds long

The vestry
The altar

The altar The North Chappell

A Pew

M.r Risley's seat   The Rector's

M.r Chetwode's Seat

The South Chappell Now a Chamber

Stair case

The Parlour

The Hall

The quier

The font

The Crosse

The Churchyard

Here a screen or partition of Timber but now a Stone Wall

This wall closes up to the Steple

This wall standeth

The Cloysters

Chambers & Lodgings

South

The well

A place for Crewets

Here stood the font but now tis removed

The Steeple

The Stable

Weste   Here cometh the Highway

Chetwode. Scheme of the Priory taken from an old one in Queen Elizabeth's time.

Plan of Chetwode priory made in the reign of Queen Elizabeth I showing that the nave of the priory church once extended to the boundary of the road and had a transept and cloister court (now gone) on the south side. The original of this drawing is now in the Bodleian Library, Oxford.

The interior of the east end of the priory church lit by three original windows. The east window has five stepped lancets and the windows in the north and south walls three lancets. In 1842, medieval glass surviving in the east window was inserted in the lancets of the south window. The glass dates from 1260-1280 and is some of the earliest in England.

This corbel near the pulpit probably represents the crowned head of Henry III.

Panel showing the Royal Arms of Henry III probably made in 1260-1280 to commemorate the King's gift of land for the building of the priory. It is the earliest known representation of the Royal Arms in stained glass in England and shows *'gules, three leopards passant guardant or.'* It was lent to the Royal Academy of Arts in London in 1987 for the exhibition *'The Age of Chivalry, Art in Plantagenet England 1200-1400.'*

The Royal Arms and two figures represented in medieval stained glass at Chetwode, illustrated in Daniel and Samuel Lysons's *Magna Britannia* (Bedfordshire, Berkshire and Buckinghamshire), 1806.

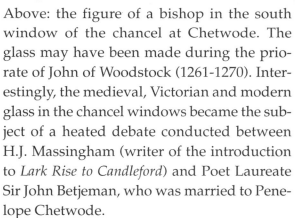

Above: the figure of a bishop in the south window of the chancel at Chetwode. The glass may have been made during the priorate of John of Woodstock (1261-1270). Interestingly, the medieval, Victorian and modern glass in the chancel windows became the subject of a heated debate conducted between H.J. Massingham (writer of the introduction to *Lark Rise to Candleford*) and Poet Laureate Sir John Betjeman, who was married to Penelope Chetwode.

Right: Victorian glass in the east window made by William Holland of Warwick in 1842.

Four Sedilia arches above three wall seats and a doorway in the south wall of the chancel. The wall seats were used by the Augustinian canons officiating at services. All of the arches are carved with stiff-leaf and dog tooth ornament.

Mr Rowland Herring holding open a trapdoor in the floor of Chetwode church to reveal the oldest monument in the building, a large grave slab to the memory of Sir John Giffard, who died in c1350. He was a member of the Twyford branch of the Giffard family, who were related to the Dukes of Normandy and were made Earls of Buckingham after the Norman Conquest. Sir John lived at Twyford manor house, for which he obtained a licence to build an Oratory (house chapel).

Drawing of the tomb slab of Sir John Giffard, illustrated in *Records of Buckinghamshire,* Vol. III (1863-67). The slab is decorated with an elaborate cross bordered by an inscription in medieval French. Also illustrated are medieval tiles from a tiled floor found near the slab, decorated with the Hapsburg Eagle (commemorating Richard of Cornwall's accession as King of the Romans) and the Royal Arms. They are identical in design to tiles found at Bicester Priory in 1965. Bicester Priory is known to have been in regular contact with Chetwode.

13th century medieval wall painting in a recess in the north wall of the chancel depicting foliage.

Hatchments hanging on the north wall of Chetwode church belonging to the Risley family, who lived at Priory House in the 17th and 18th centuries on the site of the former cloister. The hatchments represent the arms of Henry Risley, who was killed at Brest in 1682, his wife, Elizabeth, née Duncombe, Paul Risley, who died in 1738, and Risley Brewer Risley, Sheriff of Buckinghamshire, who died in 1755. The hatchments were restored by the family in 1984.

The squire's pew below the arch near the pulpit. In the 19th century the squire and his family were kept warm by a fire contained in a specially built fireplace situated in the north-west corner of the transept beyond the arch.

TWYFORD

Although she would not have known it, Flora Thompson's family had a connection with Twyford long before her uncle Thomas Whiting (*Uncle Tom* the shoemaker), moved there around 1877.

The Lambourne family are connected to Flora Thompson through the marriage of her great-great-grandfather Edward Wallington of Ludgershall to Clemence Lambourne in 1770. One of her notable ancestors was John Lambourne of Waddesdon, gentleman, who lived from about 1460 to 1540. He was a noted lawyer, acting in London for wealthy clients from Berkshire, Buckinghamshire and Oxfordshire, and from 1482-3 served as deputy sheriff for Buckinghamshire. He was the second-wealthiest person living in Waddesdon after the Countess of Devon. He rented Westcott Manor from the Crown and Crockwell Close from Bicester Priory and left several legacies to support the poor, including 20s for the poor of Bicester and 3s 4d for those of Grendon Underwood.

John's eldest son William married Jane Giffard, aunt of Roger Giffard, who was a physician to Elizabeth I. Jane was previously married to Ambrose Dauncey and in her will of 1558 left a valuable table carpet to her son William Dauncey, which is now displayed in the Victoria & Albert Museum.

Hugh, probably the youngest son of John Lambourne, gentleman (Flora's nine times great-grandfather), was born in c1490 and buried in Goddington church in 1569. He left the largest of the Lambourne wills, leaving items to his three sons: William (born c1520), John born c1550 (Flora's ancestor) and Henry. William's legacy included cattle, geldings, 400 sheep and a Sapphire stone 'that his grandfather gave him'.

Hugh's son John was the first to move to Charndon, a hamlet of Twyford, around 1570. He probably lived in Dunsty Hill Farm, which the family occupied until about 1670, when they moved to Ludgershall. In his will of 1596 John was described as a yeoman and specifically requested to be buried in Twyford church. In her will proved in 1612 his widow Margaret bequeathed a great cupboard in the kitchen to her son Thomas. There are other wills of the Lambournes of Charndon which reveal the occupations of the family: Christopher, who died in 1698, was a ploughwright, Thomas (died in 1735) was a husbandman, John (died 1752) was a yeoman, John (died 1799) was a dairyman and William Lambourne (died 1840) was a shopkeeper in Twyford. Several of the wills include the bequest of a set of silver spoons with acorn tops which may have been made in the 15th century.

The main manor in Twyford was dominated by two families. The Giffard family held land in Twyford from about 1276, amalgamating two manors there around 1440, which passed to the Wenmans through Ursula Giffard's marriage to Sir Thomas Wenman in 1520. The Wenmans, who were originally clothiers of Witney, held it until Philip, the last Viscount Wenman, died in 1800, when the manor passed to a nephew, William Wykeham. Ferdinando Wenman, who was born at Twyford, was closely involved with the doomed English settlement of Jamestown in America, being appointed as General of the Horse for life in the revised charter of 1609, and later referred to as a Marshal.

Thomas Whiting, Flora's *Uncle Tom*, was born in Roade, Northamptonshire, in 1850, the son of Austin Masters Whiting, but after his father (who had started his career as a wool and linen draper and descended to being a hawker) emigrated alone to America, leaving his wife and family behind, Tom spent some of his childhood in Cottisford, living with his maternal grandparents Thomas and Harriet Batchelor. Although Thomas was an agricultural labourer, Tom set himself up as a shoemaker, and was living in Juniper Hill in 1871. He must have become friendly with Flora's family as a young man, as he was a witness at the wedding of Flora's parents Albert Timms and Emma Dibber in 1875. He married Albert's sister Ann Timms in Buckingham on 17 April 1876. Their first daughter Mary Martha was born in Cottisford, but his other children were born after his move to Twyford: Ellen Jane in 1878, Anne Elizabeth in 1880, Amy in 1882 and John Austin Whiting in 1885. In a 1910 survey of Twyford he was living in what was then Chilton Place, now designated School Lane, in a cottage with a garden. This is probably the same house he had been living in since he moved to Twyford. Whether or not his shop was on the same premises is not known – directory entries only list him as a shoemaker and do not give his address. Flora Thompson described the shop as being the last in the street with a shop window displaying a lady's boot on a velvet cushion with a signboard reading: *'Ladies boots and shoes made to order. Best Materials. Perfect Workmanship. Fit Guaranteed. Ladies Hunting Boots a Speciality'*. Flora implies in *Lark Rise to Candleford* that he worked in *Candleford*, and it has been suggested that she aggrandised his business so that it was more like the shoe factory of Rechab Holland in Buckingham, but the character she described was definitely that of her real Uncle Thomas. He was better off than her father and, when Flora went to stay, she could browse through his fascinating cache of books in the attic. He may have been the first to recognise Flora's potential and encourage her.

Flora would have spent time with her cousins. Martha Mary, nick named *Molly* in *Lark Rise to Candleford*, but really known as Polly. She went into domestic service and became a cook in Oxford, marrying groom Edwin Cherry in 1901. Ellen (Nellie) married railway porter William John Bryan. Anne (Annie) became a cook and married John Beckett, an agricultural labourer. Amy became a house parlour maid and Johnny was working with Thomas as a shoemaker in 1901 but, according to Flora, became a soldier in the First World War and spent time as a prisoner of war.

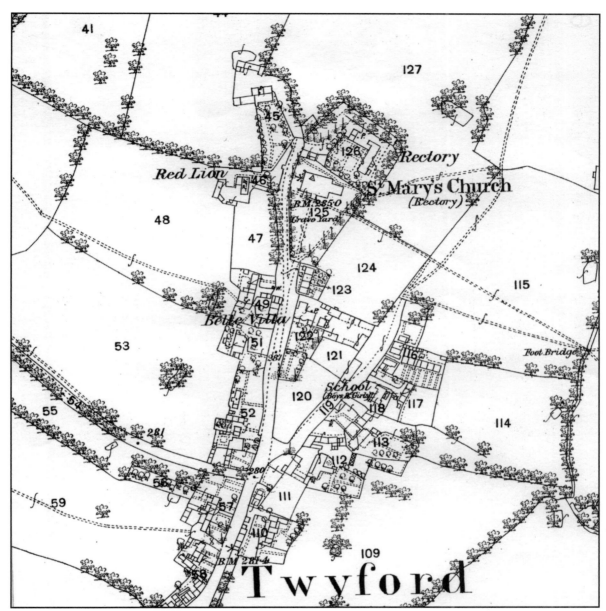

Ordnance Survey map showing Twyford in 1880. The ancient centre of the village, marked by the parish church, the rectory and the *Red Lion* public house, is now a dead end, as a former ancient route northward to Preston Bissett was effectively blocked in the 19th century by the building of the Great Central Railway.

Twyford church looking north. The church, consisting of a nave, north and south aisles, chancel, porch and west tower, dates back to the 12th century. The graveyard contains the bodily remains of a large number of Flora Thompson's Lambourne ancestors, who lived in the parish from c1570 until c1670, when Flora's branch of the family moved to Ludgershall. The Twyford hamlet of Poundon, situated on the top of Poundon Hill next to the former signal station, was home to another branch of Flora's ancestral family headed by Vincent Smith and his wife Elizabeth, née Shaw, of Piddington. Vincent Smith operated as a clockmaker in the 1730s, and specialised in making turret clocks for local churches.

The 13th century effigy of Sir William de Fougères, a former lord of the manor, wearing a pot helmet and chain mail, in the south aisle of Twyford church. He was a descendent of Ralph de Fougères, who was the lord of the manor at the time of the Domesday Book.

Palimpsest brass to the memory of Thomas Giffard, who died in 1550, set in a slab of Purbeck marble on top of an earlier 15th century Giffard table tomb, situated next to the effigy of Sir William de Fougères. Thomas's daughter, Ursula, married Sir Thomas Wenman, whose family remained lords of the manor in Twyford until the 20th century. Flora Thompson had a distant family connection with the Wenmans and Giffards. Thomas Giffard's first cousin, Jane Giffard, married William Lambourne of Waddesdon, gentleman, and is buried in the choir of Middle Claydon church next to Claydon House. William's younger brother Hugh Lambourne, (c1490-1569), gentleman, of Oldfields Copse Farm in Goddington, was the ten times great-grandfather of Flora Thompson.

Family tree illustrating Flora Thompson's relationship to the influential Lambourne, Giffard and Wenman families.

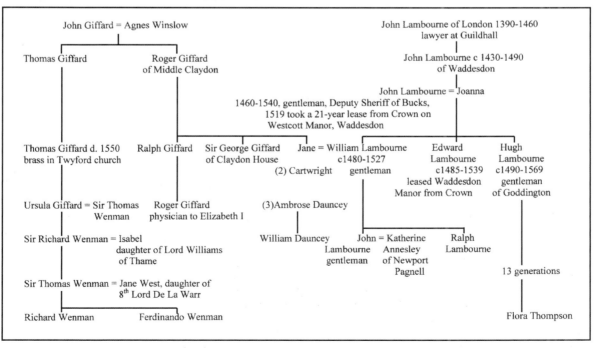

The wall monument to Richard, first Viscount Wenman/Waineman,who died in 1640, blocks the former east window in the south aisle. Richard's great-grandmother was Ursula Giffard. He was knighted for gallantry after the seige of Cadiz and was awarded a Viscountcy in 1628. Another noteworthy member of the local Wenman family was Ferdinando who took a leading part in the colonial settlement of Jamestown, Virginia, in the early 17th century.

The former rectory behind the church is one of the oldest and most interesting buildings in Twyford. The oldest part is half-timbered and began life in the mid 15th century as a hall and solar. A 16th century extension received panelling and a staircase, which still survives.

The former Red Lion public house opposite the church and rectory, with the last landlord Colin Thompson and John Watts standing outside before it closed in the 1990s. The building dates back to the 17th century and had functioned as a public house since the middle of the 18th century. Victuallers licensing records show that John Clayton served as an early licensee from c1756 to c1790.

Here in the background at the north end of School Lane stands the former red-brick house and shop of Thomas Whiting, Flora's *Uncle Tom*, who moved to Twyford in c1877 and worked as a shoemaker specialising in making hunting boots. Flora Thompson may have lodged here with her uncle and aunt for a few months in 1895 when she left Fringford to work at Twyford's old Post Office, which was located a few doors away.

Entry in the Buckingham parish register recording the marriage of Thomas James Whiting (*Uncle Tom*) and Ann Elizabeth Timms at Buckingham on 17 April 1876 with the signatures of Flora's parents Albert and Emma Timms, who both acted as witnesses.

The old Post Office, where Flora Thompson is believed to have worked briefly in 1895, before taking up a new post office job at Grayshott in Hampshire.

Poundon and Marsh Gibbon railway station (on the London and North-Western Railway line which connected Oxford to Bletchley, Bedford and Cambridge) was situated halfway between Twyford and Marsh Gibbon on the Marsh Gibbon road. The next stations down the line were Launton and Bicester. Here the station is seen with a train carrying coal over the Poundon railway bridge.

MARSH GIBBON

The village has Anglo-Saxon origins but the name 'Gibbon' comes from the Gibbewin family who held a manor in Marsh in the 12th century. A larger manor of over 1000 acres was granted to the Earl of Mortain at the Conquest and held from him by the Norman Abbey of Grestain until 1348, when it was demised to the king's merchant Tideman de Lymbergh. Two years later it was transferred to Michael, Thomas and Edmund de la Pole. This link with the de la Pole family has had a strong continuing influence over the village. In 1437 William de la Pole, Duke of Suffolk, and his wife Alice (the grand-daughter of the poet Geoffrey Chaucer) established an almshouse at Ewelme and the manor of Marsh was endowed to it. The almshouse survived the Dissolution, probably because Henry VIII was its patron. Under James I the mastership of Ewelme Almshouse was assigned to the Regius Professor of Medicine at the University of Oxford.

Sir Henry Acland, who became Regius Professor of Medicine in 1856, was so horrified to find the village in a derelict state that he instituted major improvements which were completed about 1890. He wrote a book entitled *Health in the Village* which described the appalling conditions, disguising the village under the name of *Lowmarsh* and the Greyhound public house as *The Bulldog*. J.B. Atley in *Henry Acland: A Memoir* described the conditions:

Half ruined cottages, a grey old Elizabethan manor house drifting into decay, a shallow pit of brown pear-coloured water, serving as the reservoir for the inhabitants and as the common drinking ground of the sheep and cattle. A knot of dwellings ... stood in the midst of a tiny sea of dark brown slush. Against each of them leaned its pigsty, and the muck-sodden floor of the lower room was scarcely less crazy than the gaping planks of the upper story.

Access to the upper storey was usually by rickety ladder and twelve people might sleep together in a room measuring ten feet by twelve. This affected the character of the inhabitants, described by Acland as being sullen. They had also been adversely affected by a disastrous fire in 1740, which began in a brew house and destroyed thirty-six houses. An appeal was sent out for aid:

Whereas a Dreadful Fire on the 6th of June last, consumed the greatest Part of Marsh Gibbon in the county of Bucks, with all or most of the Wearing Apparel, Household Furniture and Implements of Husbandry, and all the Corn and Hay of the said Inhabitants to the Value of about 7000l. and they being true Objects of Charity, We whose Names are hereunto sub-

scribed do attest the Truth thereof, and beg the timely Assistance of all charitable People, to Persons who have been always ready when call'd upon to assist others in the like distress'd Circumstances.

N.B. The Inhabitants have endeavoured to rebuild their Habitation, but find themselves incapable without Assistance.

Alex. Croke, W. Guy, Jos. Box

Enclosure in 1841 aggravated the situation by reducing labourers' rights. Acland encouraged the other trustees of the Ewelme Almshouses, who included the Dukes of Marlborough and Buckingham and the Earls of Jersey and Macclesfield, to support him in improving their plight. Prince Leopold was invited to accompany Dr Acland on a visit to Marsh Gibbon to view the new model cottages on 21 May 1875 and *Jackson's Oxford Journal* reported:

… A large number of the old cottages have been pulled down and replaced by new ones of a very superior class. Special care has been taken with regard to their sanitary arrangements, under the able superintendence of Dr. Acland, whose interest in such matters is well known. Prince Leopold examined carefully both the old and the new tenements in all their details. He was also interested in the pillow lace making and made purchases from many of the girls who still carry on this trade, though it affords them but a bare subsistence…

Lacemaking had been the principal occupation of labourers' wives and daughters in Marsh Gibbon for many years, having been introduced to the East Midlands in the 16th century. Eighteen lacemakers were recorded in the 1841 census, between the ages of 15 and 60, and there were 93 in 1861, the youngest aged 8 and the oldest 67. Strangely, not one was mentioned in the 1851 census (could they all have gone to look at the lace in the Great Exhibition on census day?). Acland described the cramped lace schools (one was a room nine feet by eight, with thirteen children seated at their pillows). Richard Heritage (1803-1865), an innkeeper in Marsh Gibbon, recorded the days in his diary when two lacemen rented a room from him (about once a month in 1852) and purchased black and white lace, each on separate days, from local women. On 14 November 1854 he recorded: '*Laceman here Great many women.*'

The Heritage family played an important role in the history of the Friendly Societies in Marsh Gibbon. The main one is the Greyhound Club, founded in 1788 by the village bell-ringers, which celebrates Oak Apple Day, 29 May, and the second one was the Coote Club, which operated from 1846 until about 1937. Friendly Societies were formed in the days before pensions and social security; members paid a small sum each week and received financial help in times of sickness and need.

As licensee of the Greyhound, Richard Heritage hosted the Club for several years. The Greyhound Club account books give fascinating insights. Members were expected to wear scarves at other members' funerals and supplies of these were kept in a box ready for use. The Club had a banner which was carried in procession; in 1823 John Heritage was paid £3 17s 7d for painting and gilding flags and staves. The Musician was given a contribution of £1 towards the purchase of a drum in 1823.

1888 was a momentous year with two celebrations. The 100th Club Day was held on 29 May 1888: the members went to church and then had a dinner. Thirty-six yards of ribbon were purchased for the occasion and £6 1s 11d was spent on meat, 11s 7d on bread and flour and £1 2s 3d on grocery. The Brill band paraded the village and eighteen gallons of beer were given away.

A second celebration was held at the Greyhound on 6 October 1888 to commemorate the centenary of the foundation of the Club. This time music was provided by the Marsh Gibbon band and dinner was provided with beer and ginger beer. Richard Shirley, who had served as clerk of the club for thirty-three years, was presented with a silver cruet. There were speeches and songs, stalls were set out and beer and tobacco provided.

Few places apart from Marsh Gibbon still celebrate Oak Apple Day (which commemorated Charles II hiding in the Boscobel oak during his escape after defeat at the Battle of Worcester). Today the celebrations are held on the Saturday closest to 29 May. People process to church and then a feast is held in the village hall.

Box Farm

The recent history of farming in Marsh Gibbon is typical of this part of Buckinghamshire: many small farms have ceased to exist and their land has been absorbed into larger units. In Marsh Gibbon several tenant farmers retired in the 1960s, so the Ewelme Trust amalgamated holdings, reducing the number of farms from the seventeen found before the Second World War to five.

Box Farm, formerly owned by the Ewelme Trust, is situated in Castle Street by the former Red Lion public house. The thatched Elizabethan stone farmhouse had a farmyard, rickyard and orchard behind it and 120 acres of fields, mostly in Station Road. It was tenanted in the 18th and 19th centuries by the Box family and their Mason relatives and, from around 1875 to 1961, by three generations of the Judge family. The farmhouse was sold in 1971, following Bernard Judge's death in 1970.

Dairying provided the main income. In 1910 the Judges had eight Shorthorn cows (suitable for milk and beef), which were hand-milked. About nine gallons of milk were sold daily to villagers who brought their own cloth-covered jugs, at 2d per pint or 16d a gallon. The remainder was processed by United Dairies in Buckingham. In the 1950s an electric milking machine was purchased, enabling Brian Judge to keep 16 shorthorns.

Four twenty-ton ricks of hay were built each year for winter feed and excess hay was sold to London dealers and to the Carter and Heritage families, who made straw ropes. Hay and straw were carted in two yellow painted Oxfordshire wagons with red wheels and black lettering.

There was no arable farming between the wars, but a flock of 30-40 breeding ewes was kept. Dipping was done in Arthur John Willoughby Phipps's dip at Westbury Manor. Until the early 1900s wool was sold at Bicester Wool Fair. Later the Judges sold fleeces to H.C. Pierce, the woolstapler from Thame. The Judges kept a sow and two piglets; the latter were fattened for making hams. Brewing was done on the farm in a 70-gallon copper in the brewhouse until the early 20th century. The family did most of the farm work themselves, augmented by Italian and German prisoners of war and land girls during the Second World War. After the war casual labourers were employed and half the farm was arable, growing wheat and dredge corn (a mixture of wheat, barley and oats) for cattle feed. The land has now been amalgamated with that of Manor Farm.

The 'Ewelme' manor house situated south-west of the parish church at Marsh Gibbon. The central 16th century hall may incorporate parts of the earlier medieval manor house once used by the de le Pole family. On the death of Thomas de le Pole in 1418, one-third of the manor of Marsh Gibbon was assigned in dower for his widow Anne, including one-third of the manor house, which was described as being *'two bays in the west of the hall, with free entry and exit, one bay and a half of a grange therein to the north, and one third of the profits of a dovehouse'*. Following the death of Thomas de la Pole, junior, aged 13, in 1429, the house and manor passed to his cousin William de la Pole, later Duke of Suffolk. William and his wife Alice, née Chaucer, had close family contacts with the Rede family of Boarstall Tower, who were descended from William's uncle Edmund de la Pole, Captain of Calais.

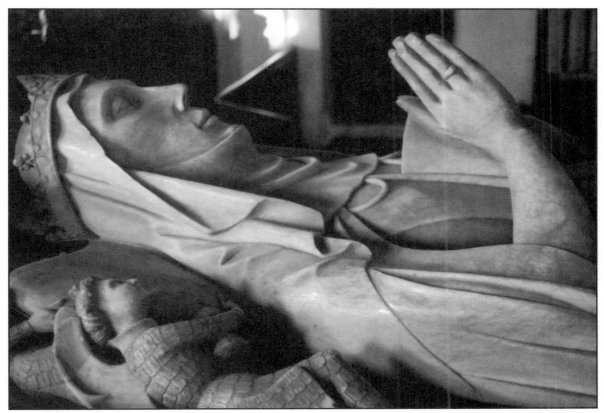

The magnificent alabaster effigy in Ewelme church of Alice, Duchess of Suffolk, née Chaucer, who married William de la Pole in 1437. The Ewelme almshouses and school were set up at the request of King Henry VI because Alice Chaucer was the King's ward and William had married her without the King's consent. To fund the maintenance of the almshouses, William and Alice were obliged to give two manors, one of which was Marsh Gibbon, acquired by the de la Pole family in about 1350. (Courtesy of Martin Haslett)

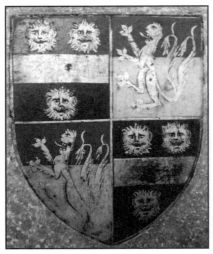

Shield placed by Alice de la Pole on the tomb of her father Thomas Chaucer at Ewelme. It bears the de la Pole arms: *azure a fesse between three leopards' faces or*, quartering Burghersh: *argent a chief gules with a double-tailed lion or over all*. Alice de la Pole was the daughter of Maud Burghersh and the granddaughter of Sir John Burghersh of Ewelme. (Courtesy of Martin Haslett)

The grammar school built in c1442 at Ewelme, maintenance of which was later funded by the rents of the de la Pole manor at Marsh Gibbon. (Courtesy of Martin Haslett)

Thatched cottages in Castle Street before their demolition in the early 1870s to make way for the new model houses built by the Ewelme Trust. The programme of demolition and the replacement of tumbledown properties with new model houses was led by Sir Henry Acland, Professor of Medicine at Oxford and Master of the Ewelme Trust, who was appalled at the unwholesome living conditions endured by many of Marsh Gibbon's inhabitants when he first visited the village in the 1860s.

A drawing made of the living conditions endured by many of the poor of Marsh Gibbon in the 1860s. (Courtesy of the Centre for Buckinghamshire Studies)

Model houses built in Castle Street by the Ewelme Trust replacing the many mud and thatch one-up-and-one-down cottages in Castle Street and Summerstown at the eastern end of the village.

Drawing of the interior of a lace school operating at Marsh Gibbon in the 1860s. Several lace schools taught the art of lacemaking to children and young adults. One operated in a thatched cottage in the 'College' area immediately north of the parish church; another was located at Forge House on the corner of Clements Lane. Many of the older women in the village were highly skilled in the art of Buckinghamshire lace making, which served as a useful supplement to income. (Courtesy of the Centre for Buckinghamshire Studies).

Mrs Hine making Buckinghamshire lace outside her Ewelme almshouse in Clements Lane, Marsh Gibbon, in 1900. The North Buckinghamshire Lace Association was set up in 1897 to revive lacemaking in Buckinghamshire. (Courtesy of Mrs Eileen Chambers)

Portrait of publican Richard Heritage (1803-1865) taken by a travelling photographer who visited Marsh Gibbon and nearby Blackthorn in 1862. Richard Heritage was licensee of the *White Hart* in Church Street (and for a few years *The Greyhound*) and left a detailed diary, which records that in the 1850s he regularly rented out a room once a month to two lace buyers who visited the village on different days, using the room as a base to buy white and black lace from villagers and to sell them lace cottons in return. The late Harriett Ellen Waddup, glovemaker, of Marsh Gibbon (1906-2006) recalled that in the early 1900s the lacemen came from Banbury and sold the lace to specialist lace shops in London. (Courtesy of the Centre for Buckinghamshire Studies)

Members of the Marsh Gibbon Greyhound Club assembled outside the *Greyhound* public house in 1898 to celebrate the 110th anniversary of the foundation of the society.

A new member of the Marsh Gibbon Greyhound Club being initiated by drinking a large measure of beer from the Society's 1788 metal jug outside the *Greyhound* public house on the evening of Club day c1970. (Courtesy of the Centre for Buckinghamshire Studies, Cutforth Collection)

The village band leading the procession of the Greyhound Friendly Society to the service held at the church on Club day 1898. On the left is the cottage, wheelwright's and painter's shop belonging to village wheelwright, Reginald Simms, and, on the right, an old thatched barn belonging to Home Farm. In the distance can be seen Tompkins's (later Isaac Parker's) grocers' shop, the side wall of which carries an advert for Lux soap.

The procession of members of Marsh Gibbon's two main friendly societies, the Greyhound Club and the Coote Club, to Marsh Gibbon church on 29 May 1937. The banner carried in front of the band reads at the top 'COOTE CLUB FRIENDLY SOCIETY 1846'. The whitewashed building in the background is the 16th century *Plough Inn* and the wall on the right marked the eastern boundary to the grounds of the manor house owned by the de la Pole family. (Courtesy of the Centre for Buckinghamshire Studies, Cutforth collection)

The cover of the rules of the Marsh Gibbon Coote Club Friendly Society, established in 1846. The rules were printed by Smith and Pankhurst at their printing works in the Market Place, Bicester, in 1882. (Courtesy of the Centre for Buckinghamshire Studies)

The thatched farmhouse of Box Farm, situated near the junction of Church Street with Castle Street, which appears to have been tenanted in the 18th and 19th centuries by the Box family (and their Mason relatives), who had their origins in Launton and Bicester. Possibly the most illustrious member of the family was Philip Box, who was born at Bicester in 1740 and founded the Buckingham Box Bank in 1786. The bank (now part of Lloyds) had offices in Buckingham's town hall and issued its own bank notes.

George Judge (1846-1905), farmer of Box Farm from c1875 to 1905. He died of peritonitis at the age of 59 and the farm was then run by his wife Anne, née Shaw, and their youngest son Bernard.

Anne Judge (1851-1916), farmer of Box Farm, photographed shortly after her marriage to George Judge at Ambrosden in 1875. Anne's father, George Shaw (butcher, of Blackthorn), was the best man at the wedding of Flora Thompson's grandparents Thomas and Martha Timms at Ambrosdon in 1844.

The rear of Box Farm farmhouse with Bernard Judge and his wife Doris, standing at the wicket gate next to the dairy (right) in c1920. The external stone staircase on the left led to the granary, which was immediately above the flag-stoned pantry and kitchen. Above the granary there was an attic in which fleeces were annually stored in a bin after sheep shearing on the farm in May. The bin held forty fleeces and by providing airtight conditions, stopped the grease in the wool from drying out.

Farmer Bernard Judge (1890-1970) and his wife Doris, née Gordon, a Marsh Gibbon school-teacher at the time of their marriage in 1917. Bernard Judge lived all his life at Box Farm where he maintained a small herd of sixteen red and white Shorthorn cows, which were walked twice a day at 6 a.m. and 3 p.m. from the meadows in Station Road to the milking shed in the farm yard. The cows each produced an average of three gallons of milk daily.

Anne Judge feeding her hens in Box Farm farmyard in 1906, photographed by Frederick Holmdon White, cartoonist for *Punch* magazine. Eggs provided a useful supplement to the farm's income and in the 1940s and 1950s fifty hens were kept in eight hen coops in the rickyard. As well as selling eggs to a visiting eggler (normally Crook and Son of Waddesdon), the farm produced up to a hundred hens and cockerels annually for sale at Christmas.

May Chandler standing in the rick yard at Box Farm in August 1906. Behind her stand two Oxfordshire farm wagons and two of the farm's four hayricks. The newly-built rick on the right is protected by a rick sheet, which was supported on a rope raised by a pulley. Rick sheets were kept raised above hayricks to prevent condensation, which led to the dangerous growth of mould.

Brian Judge dressed in a khaki cowgown cutting cakes of hay from a rick behind the milking shed at Box Farm in the late 1940s. Each cake weighed over 30 kilos (70 pounds) and a cow could eat up to twelve cakes of hay a day in winter.

Farmer Bernard Judge, Samuel Crowcombe and Brian Judge riding in a trap in Box Farm farmyard, behind the farmhouse, in 1935. The farmyard's thatched manger holding small quantities of hay for waiting horses stands in the background. An almost identical manger stood in the farmyard at Stonewalls Farm at Chalfont St. Giles, in the early 1900s.

George Heritage, Herbert Spiers and Jim White, with cider flagons in a trap in Box Farm farmyard in the 1930s, before going harvesting in Station Road.

Milk from Box Farm and other local farms being loaded on to a lorry at Marsh Gibbon for delivery to the United Dairies' Creamery at Buckingham.

Farmer Thomas Judge, brother of George Judge of Box Farm. Thomas Judge served as a district councillor and farmed at Gubbins Hole Farm, between Marsh Gibbon and Grendon Underwood, from c1900 until his death in 1933. Gubbins Hole Farm was a part of the Westbury Manor and derived its name Gubbins from the Gibwen or Gibbons family, who held the manor in the 12th century. They also gave their name to the village, which prior to their tenure was known as Merse.

The front of Gubbins Hole Farm farmhouse, built of variegated brick, in the winter of 1910. A potato clamp protected by a roof of plaited straw is visible on the left.

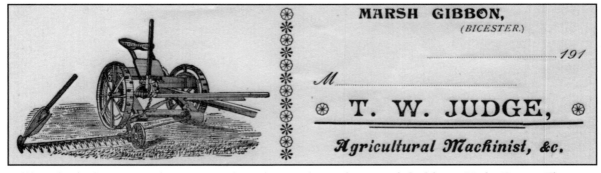

Billhead of Thomas Judge, Agriculturalist and Machinist of Gubbins Hole Farm. Thomas Judge and his son Thomas Judge, junior, operated a thrashing box driven by a small portable steam engine, which they took to farms in the Marsh Gibbon area for threshing corn in the spring.

Mr Joby Reeves photographed with the giant cart-horse *Scylax* at Richard Joseph Rigby's farm at Souldern, Oxfordshire. The postcard advertising the cart-horse was sent by Mr Rigsby to Thomas Judge at Gubbins Hole Farm in 1907. The message on the back reads:

'*Dear Sir,*

Try another horse. If she stands to wagons I shall trust you to pay. If not I shall expect nothing. If you were here you would appreciate our difficulty through the new line (construction of the Aynho to Princes Risborough section of the Great Western Railway through the Souldern valley).
Yours truly,

R.J. Rigsby'
(Courtesy of Henry Westbury)

Florence Judge of Gubbins Hole Farm with her donkey cart making her weekly collection of bread and cakes from Baldwins' bakehouse in Castle Street, Marsh Gibbon c.1905.

Across the fields from Gubbins Hole Farm is the former *Ship Inn* at Grendon Underwood where William Shakespeare occasionally broke his journey from London to Stratford. Local tradition has it that he used to rent the main upstairs room (which still survives) at the *Ship*, some two hundred yards from the parish church. John Aubrey, wrote in *Brief Lives*: '*The Humour of the Constable in* **Midsomer's Night Dream** *he happened to take at Grendon in Bucks (I think it was on Midsomer Night that he happened to lye there) which is the road from London to Stratford, and there was living that constable about 1642, when I first came to Oxon.*' Another version of the Shakespeare connection was recorded in the 19th century by Aylesbury historian, Robert Gibbs, who maintained that Shakespeare fell asleep in Grendon church porch and was arrested by the two parish constables for being there. He then mischievously cast them as the two constables, *Dogberry* and *Verges*, in his play *Much Ado about Nothing*. There is an-

other village tradition that Shakespeare used to walk in the woods around Grendon Underwood. Perhaps significantly, local people within living memory could point to the existence of large grassy mounds in one wood on which wild thyme grew - a subject used by Shakespeare in his *A Midsummer Night's Dream*.

LAUNTON

The manor of Launton was presented by Edward the Confessor, who was born in Islip, to his new foundation of the Abbey of St Peter at Westminster in 1065. Manorial records state that the Abbey employed a bailiff to run the estate, supported by a reeve, four ploughmen, a carter, a cowherd, a shepherd and a female servant. The bailiff lived in a thatched manor house in 1267, with a ground-floor hall and chamber above. Outbuildings included a bake-house, dairy, cow shed and granary. Sometimes they also paid a smith, miller and swineherd and sometimes an additional female servant. Additional labourers were taken on in the spring for harrowing and a reap-reeve was employed for six or eight weeks at harvest, and sometimes another shepherd in the summer. Full-time servants were paid mostly in corn and a common table was sometimes provided at Christmas and between 1 August and 29 September for the bailiff, reeve and female servants. Much of the labour was done by customary tenants. In 1416 there were eleven customary tenants with a virgate of land, three with half-virgates, six tenants with composite holdings and sixteen leaseholders. The manor house became Manor Farm, tenanted by the Oakley family from 1663 to 1723.

In 1650 the house had been rebuilt with a hall, panelled parlour, kitchen, buttery, larder, wash house, four chambers used as bedrooms, a chamber for storing corn, two other chambers, two cock lofts and a mill house. Manor courts were held here and a new wing was built to house them in 1823. The last member of the Oakley family, who died in 1723, is reputed to haunt the house, dressed in everyday clothes with a high crowned-hat and mittens. The lease passed to the Earl of Jersey.

When the parish was enclosed in 1814, the principal award was made to Lord Jersey, with five other awards of over 100 acres and five over 30 acres. Twenty-six proprietors received awards but twenty-eight others who owned only cottages and small closes received nothing.

Flora Thompson was fascinated by the gypsies, and would have been intrigued by the note Robert Gibbs wrote in *A Record of Local Occurrences in Buckinghamshire*, Vol. III (1880):

13th February 1830

'Old James Smith, the Gypsy King, died a fortnight ago at Launton; he was 100 years old, and has left a widow of even greater age; the poor old woman was almost frantic on the loss of her husband. They had 16 children; grandchildren and great grandchildren, innumerable. The old folks belonged to Wendlebury, in which parish the old man was born in a gipsy's tent.'

Population increased during the 19th century from 372 in 1801 to 706 in 1851 and 746 in 1871. There was some poverty and in 1852 the Bicester Board of Guardians tried to ameliorate this situation by sanctioning payment of £32 to any Launton resident who decided to emigrate to Australia. They also offered money to potential emigrants to Canada, but the offers were not always taken up.

The Rectory was built in the 16th and 17th centuries. Henry Rowlands, the incumbent from 1581 to 1600, planted a yew hedge which was damaged by fire in 1716 and repaired. The Revd James Blomfield, who was Rector from 1838 to1842, spent £1500, half of which was borrowed from Queen Anne's Bounty, enlarging the Rectory, making it a two-storey rectangular building, containing earlier features such as an 18th century staircase and 17th and 18th century panelling. He set up a new Church of England school in 1838, badly needed as the Earl of Jersey had sold his land in Launton around 1826 and Lady Jersey had withdrawn the support she had given to the local school so it was forced to close. Not all parents wanted their children educated by the Church of England, so a Congregational School was set up in 1845, meeting in the Zion chapel until a new school was built in 1852. Blomfield later became Rector of Orsett in Essex and his son, Canon James Charles Blomfield, who attended Exeter College, Oxford, was Rector of Launton for much of the second half of the 19th century, from 1850 until 1895, rising to the rank of Rural Dean. He was a noted local historian, who had intended to write a history of Launton, which unfortunately never got further than notes. He kept an establishment which in 1861 included a cook, nurse, parlour maid, housemaid and groom. The Rectory had extensive grounds, which he opened up for village events such as flower shows, school treats and fetes. He was proud of his gardens and encouraged the villagers by setting up a local horticultural society.

Flora Thompson's great-aunt Clementina Wallington and her husband John Waine, who married in 1841, moved to Launton from Arncott before 1851. John was unsuccessful as a farmer and was reduced from being of independent means to becoming a farm labourer. Clementina had worked as a dressmaker and milliner in London, living with her elder sister Elizabeth in Swinton Street, Grays Inn, before her marriage and around 1871 finances must have been tight as she is recorded in the census return as pursuing that career again, whereas in other returns she is merely a labourer's wife. John and Clementina had seven sons and a daughter, Dorothy Mary Ann, who was born in 1849. Their eldest son John, born in 1842, became a successful stonemason and moved to Buckingham, Thomas Edward, born in 1846, was a wheelwright in Bicester, working for Joseph Layton, as was his younger brother Arthur Edward (born in 1863), who was a bricklayer. William Wallington Waine, born in 1852, became a painter's labourer. The only son to follow in his father's footsteps was Harry Havelock, born in 1859, who became a farm labourer. Clementina died in 1888 in Launton and was buried in the churchyard. Flora would have known her cousins and probably met them sometimes when she visited Bicester and Buckingham.

Launton Church, Bicester.

Launton church viewed from the south-west in 1910. The two wooden crosses in the foreground mark the graves of Flora Thompson's aunt Clementina Waine, née Wallington (died 1888), and her husband John (died 1896). The church dates back to at least 1065 when the advowson with the manor was given by Edward the Confessor to Westminster Abbey. The Anglo-Saxon church is believed to have had an apse, the foundation walls of which survive under the floor of the present chancel. The west tower and side aisles were added to an existing nave early in the 13th century.

The front of Launton Rectory viewed from the Bicester Road in the early 1900s. The left side of the building (now demolished) was built in the 16th and 17th centuries and was rumoured to have had a secret room for hiding visiting priests, secretly ordained by Bishop Skinner. The main wing to the right survives and was commissioned in 1838 by the Rector James Blomfield. The builder was Oxford builder John Plowman, who also built the Bicester Workhouse. In the Second World War the building was requisitioned by the Royal Air Force and used as an Auxiliary Air Force Hostel.

The back of Launton Rectory with its well-known yew hedge photographed by Henry Taunt in 1904, which is recorded by James Blomfield as having been planted by Rector Henry Rowlands between 1581 and 1600. It was described by John Dunkin in 1823 as one of the finest and loftiest hedges in the county and is still in existence. In the 17th century the Rectory was the home of eminent cleric Bishop Skinner who was Rector of Launton between 1632 and 1663 and Bishop of Oxford from 1641 to 1663. Skinner attested that during the rule of Oliver Cromwell he had secretly ordained between 400 and 500 priests at Launton. During the Second World War, the lawn viewed here was the venue for a short play depicting an episode in the life of Bishop Skinner performed by members of the Bicester County

School. The audience included the Bishop of Oxford and the play starred James Davies as Bishop Skinner, Miss Burrows as his wife, and fifth former John Kiely as the Revd Ebenezer Scroggs. John Kiely took the part of a fiery bible-quoting puritan minister who was supported by two Cromwellian officers in uniform. Bishop Skinner's original silver communion chalice was loaned for the occasion.

The Revd James Charles Blomfield (1822-1895), Rector of Launton and Rural Dean. Blomfield, who served as Rector from 1850 to 1895, was the son of earlier Rector James Blomfield, who built Launton's Church of England School in 1838. James Charles Blomfield was a noted local historian and is best remembered for his histories of Bicester and over twenty villages and hamlets in the Bicester Deanery, published between 1882 and 1894. He planned histories for Launton and Piddington but these survive only in note form.

The pupils of Standard 5 at Launton's Church of England School photographed in 1895. Some of the very youngest children, not yet at school, were brought in specially for the occasion. Francis Abraham Harrison, who was headmaster from 1884 until he retired in 1921, is on the far left. Mrs Pat Tucker records that he was the organist and choirmaster at Launton Church for over thirty years and that he encouraged his pupils to take part in sports, particularly cricket and football. Those on the photograph have been identified as:

Front row, left to right: Herbert Jeacock, Edward Castle (holding board), Herbert Waine and William Simmonds. Second row from front, left to right: Owen Castle, Eva Jeacock, Anne Massey, Kate Castle, Stanley Harrison, Berry Harrison, Kate Cartwright, Arthur Freeman, John Massey and Richard Jeacock. Third row, left to right: Walter Holt, Lily Harrison, Ellen Castle, Edith Hazell, Kit Shrimpton, Mary Marriott (Polly), Elizabeth Waine, Sally Massey and Florence Harrison. Fourth row, left to right: Headmaster Frances Harrison, Anne Waine, Lily Simmonds, Elizabeth Herring, Nell Hazell, Eva Carter, Elizabeth Massey, Maud Harrison and Sally Marriott. Fifth row, left to right: Fred Jeacock, William Holt, Sydney Coombs, Joshua Jeacock, Carter, Freeman, Isaac Jones, Freeman and Jesse Carter.

Station road looking north from the *Bull* crossroads in 1890. Flora's aunt Clementina Waine, née Wallington, lived in the house in the foreground on the immediate right, which was then known as *The College*.

Five of the eight children of Walter Timms and his wife Sarah, née Freeman, taken outside their cottage near the Bull in c1900. Left to right, the children are: Frances (born 1894), Walter (1896-1983), Rose (born 1895), Henry (1895-1988) and Ellen (1893-1988). (Courtesy of John Jackson)

The Bull public-house at the cross-roads in Launton in c1900. It is one of the most architecturally important and imposing old buildings in the village, possibly dating back to the 16th century, as it is shown on a village map of 1607. In the 19th century it was a venue for coroners' inquests, auction sales and, on a few occasions, prize fights. Mrs Pat Tucker in *Let's Look at Launton* (1987) records that the final meeting of the Manor Court took place here in 1925 *'bringing to an end the centuries old link between Launton and the Abbey of Westminster'*. (Courtesy of Launton Historical Society)

Villagers assembled with the Launton band outside *The Bull* on Coronation Day 1902. The man seated in the centre wearing a top hat and strumming a banjo is Albert Timms's first cousin, Harry Havelock Waine (1859-1903), who was named after a Crimean war general. He was drowned in the canal at Little Woolstone, Bucks. On the extreme left are Albert Timms's first cousin, stonemason Arthur Waine (1863-1947) and his son Arthur Edward Waine, junior (1891-1978), who emigrated to Canada in 1913. He became deputy sheriff of the Algoma region in Ontario and set up a very successful gravel trucking and house moving business (using jacks and rollers) in Toronto. (Courtesy of Launton Historical Society)

Thomas Waine (1846-1918), first cousin of Flora Thompson's father Albert Timms, photographed in his wheelwright's yard at Forge Cottage, West End, Launton, shortly before dying in the flu epidemic of 1918. Thomas stands with his wife Anne, née Jeacock, and their daughter Anne, later Mrs Walker. Thomas Waine served a seven-year apprenticeship with William Parrott in Station Road, Launton, where he made the bodies of Hansom Cabs for the London market. In the 1880s he worked with his younger brother Arthur for Joseph Belsey Layton in the carpenter's shop behind Layton's shop premises on Market Hill, Bicester. In 1892 he bought the Forge, West End, Launton, from the Church Commissioners and there built Oxfordshire wagons and acted as an undertaker. He had a family of seven sons and three daughters.

Boer War veteran John Waine (1874-1940) seen in his Dragoon Guards uniform. He was a son of Thomas Waine, the Launton wheelwright and second cousin to Flora Thompson. He joined the Dragoon Guards in 1891, aged 17, and was stationed in India at Lahore until the outbreak of the Boer War. In 1899 he took part in the defence of Ladysmith and returned to England from South Africa in 1904. John's left sleeve carries two army good conduct badges surmounted by two crossed rifles, indicating that he had received a marksman's award.

Another Boer War veteran was John Waine's brother, Edward, 1876-1951 (seen here in 1903), who served in the Second Coldstream Guards. He was in the relief force that raised the siege of Ladysmith, in whose defence his brother was involved. After the Boer War, Edward undertook sentry duty outside Buckingham Palace where he was regularly seen by Launton people visiting London for the day, who liked to relate that they had seen him standing in his sentry box.

Launton villagers photographed in front of a Bristol aeroplane after it had made an emergency landing in a field near Launton Station during fog in 1911. The boy seated in front of the letter 3, with high white collar and cap, was Albert Rodney Tack, who was born in Launton in 1903. The aeroplane was one of the first to be seen in the area.

The Launton meteorite, which fell in the garden of the cottage at Folly Farm close to the Launton/Marsh Gibbon parish boundary in 1830. The meteorite weighed 1000 grams and is important astronomically as precise details of its flight and landing were witnessed visually. It is now in the Natural History Museum collection in London, having been formerly in private collections at Hartwell House and Buckingham. The Saturday edition of the Bucks Gazette published on 10 April 1830 reported that '*A meteoric stone fell at Launton, on 15th of February last, at about half past seven in the evening. The brilliant light which accompanied it was visible at a great distance; and a labourer in the employ of Mr Cross, saw the meteor descend into some newly dug earth, in his garden, which it penetrated about a foot. The explosion was very violent, and alarmed many persons; some who saw the light, and heard the report, at Twyford, about four miles distant, compared it to the rapid discharge of a triple barrelled gun.*'

The pest-house once situated in Jarvis Lane off the Launton Road, between Bicester and Launton, was one of two near Bicester which housed people suffering from infectious diseases, particularly smallpox. The pest-houses became redundant when the Isolation Hospital was built in the grounds of the Bicester Union Workhouse at Highfield, in the later 19th century.

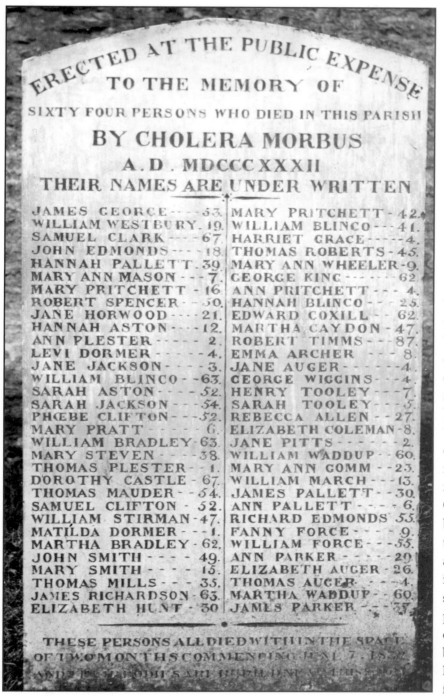

ERECTED AT THE PUBLIC EXPENSE
TO THE MEMORY OF
SIXTY FOUR PERSONS WHO DIED IN THIS PARISH
BY CHOLERA MORBUS
A.D. MDCCCXXXII
THEIR NAMES ARE UNDER WRITTEN

Name	Age	Name	Age
JAMES GEORGE	53	MARY PRITCHETT	42
WILLIAM WESTBURY	19	WILLIAM BLINCO	41
SAMUEL CLARK	67	HARRIET GRACE	4
JOHN EDMONDS	18	THOMAS ROBERTS	45
HANNAH PALLETT	39	MARY ANN WHEELER	9
MARY ANN MASON	7	GEORGE KING	62
MARY PRITCHETT	16	ANN PRITCHETT	4
ROBERT SPENCER	50	HANNAH BLINCO	25
JANE HORWOOD	21	EDWARD COXILL	62
HANNAH ASTON	12	MARTHA CAYDON	47
ANN PLESTER	2	ROBERT TIMMS	87
LEVI DORMER	4	EMMA ARCHER	8
JANE JACKSON	3	JANE AUGER	4
WILLIAM BLINCO	63	GEORGE WIGGINS	4
SARAH ASTON	52	HENRY TOOLEY	7
SARAH JACKSON	54	SARAH TOOLEY	5
PHŒBE CLIFTON	52	REBECCA ALLEN	27
MARY PRATT	6	ELIZABETH COLEMAN	8
WILLIAM BRADLEY	63	JANE PITTS	2
MARY STEVEN	38	WILLIAM WADDUP	60
THOMAS PLESTER	1	MARY ANN COMM	23
DOROTHY CASTLE	67	WILLIAM MARCH	13
THOMAS MAUDER	54	JAMES PALLETT	30
SAMUEL CLIFTON	52	ANN PALLETT	6
WILLIAM STIRMAN	47	RICHARD EDMONDS	55
MATILDA DORMER	1	FANNY FORCE	9
MARTHA BRADLEY	62	WILLIAM FORCE	55
JOHN SMITH	49	ANN PARKER	29
MARY SMITH	15	ELIZABETH AUGER	26
THOMAS MILLS	35	THOMAS AUGER	4
JAMES RICHARDSON	63	MARTHA WADDUP	60
ELIZABETH HUNT	30	JAMES PARKER	37

THESE PERSONS ALL DIED WITHIN THE SPACE
OF TWO MONTHS COMMENCING JUNE 7, 1832
AND THEIR BODIES ARE BURIED IN A PIT NEAR THIS

The cholera morbus stone near the north wall of the Tithe Barn in St Edburg's old cemetery in Bicester, which records the deaths from cholera of sixty-four people who died in Bicester in the space of two months commencing on 7 June 1832 and were buried in a pit. It has been claimed that more people died of cholera in Bicester per hundred of the population in the 1832 outbreak, than in any other town in England. The Bicester outbreak was one of a series of cholera epidemics which affected Oxfordshire and Buckinghamshire in the 1830s - the result of drinking water being infected with the Asiatic form of the disease. Outside Bicester, an outbreak of cholera at Blackthorn Hill in 1831 killed a large number of inhabitants. Bicester was also seriously affected by repeated smallpox epidemics, one of the last being in 1863 when the local pest house was filled to overflowing.

BUCKINGHAM

Buckingham is a quiet market town, which had a population of 3585 in 1881. It was closely linked with its rural hinterland and many businesses were connected with agriculture. Flora Thompson wrote that she used Buckingham as her main source for her town of *Candleford*. It was here that she visited her grandparents Martha and Thomas Timms when she was a little girl, when they lived in Gawcott Road, on the outskirts of town. Thomas had married Martha Wallington by licence at Ambrosden in 1844 and after that they moved to St Albans, where their daughter Ann Elizabeth was born in 1846. By 1851 they had moved to Buckingham, where their second daughter Jane was baptised on 5 October 1851. Flora's father Albert was born in Buckingham on 29 July 1853 and Edwin was baptised on 19 July 1855. In 1851 the family were living in North End and Thomas worked as a stonemason and Martha as a dressmaker. By 1861 they lived in Gawcott Road. The 1871 census reveals that both Albert, aged 16, and Edwin, aged 14, were working as stonemasons too. Thomas died in the Buckingham workhouse in 1880, which suggests either poverty or that he had been tended there in his last illness. His widow Martha was living alone in Gawcott Road (now called Mitre Street) in 1881, aged 65, described in the census as *'formerly dressmaker, labourer's widow'*. She later moved to Twyford to live with her daughter Ann and her husband Thomas Whiting (Flora's *Uncle Tom*), where she died of cancer in August 1886, aged 69.

As Flora was not born until 1876, she must have been very young when she visited her grandparents in Buckingham, but she described visiting relations there at a later date. These relations were probably her Waine cousins. Martha's younger sister Clementina Wallington married John Waine and they were living in Ambrosden in 1841, which may be why Martha and Thomas married there. Their eldest son John, who was born in 1842 (nine years before Albert Timms), became a stonemason and moved to Buckingham and may well have been the inspiration, or part of it, for Flora's character *James Dowland*, whom Flora described as being a builder and contractor who undertook *'Constructions, Renovations and Sanitary Work. Estimates Free.'* She described him as being: *'One of those leading spirits found at that time in every country town or village. In addition to attending to his own not inconsiderable business … he was People's Churchwarden, choirman and occasional organist, a member of every committee, and auditor of all charity accounts. But his chief interest was in the temperance movement.'*
(*Lark Rise to Candleford*, 1973 edition, page 307)

He, perhaps with Albert Timms, may have been the inspiration for the stonemason *Thomas Hearne* in *Still Glides the Stream*. John was far more successful as a stonemason than Albert, although he did not have his own business as suggested by Flora. He worked for monumental mason Henry Harrison, who at different times operated from Cow Fair, High Street, Ford Street and Hunter Street in Buckingham. John travelled throughout England to work on churches, specialising in flower and animal sculpture. His work can be seen on several gravestones dating between 1890 and 1930 in the cemetery in Brackley Road, Buckingham; he carved the Celtic cross on the top of St Bernadine's Convent in London Road, Buckingham, and according to family tradition, the font in Buckingham church. He even carved his own gravestone, which has his trademark three-dimensional flowers, including lily of the valley, roses and ferns. If he was represented by the character *James Dowland*, his enthusiasm for temperance would have put him at odds with Albert Timms, who was rather too fond of his drink, which partly led to the decline in his career.

John Waine married widow Elizabeth Fenemore, née Giles, and they had three children, Harriet Clementina, born in 1872, Elizabeth, born in 1874, and Harry Wallington Waine, born in 1878. Flora wrote about receiving handed-down clothes from richer cousins, and these may have come from the Waine family. In 1871 John and Elizabeth were living in Fleece Yard but by 1881 they had moved to a house in Mitre Street, close to that of Martha Timms. Elizabeth, although she was a butcher's daughter, worked as a boot binder.

At one time it was thought that Flora had taken Rechab Holland, the prosperous owner of a boot and shoemaking firm in Market Square in Buckingham, employing 88 men, women and children in 1871, as her inspiration for *Uncle Tom*, and she may have had him in mind when she slightly aggrandised her real uncle, Thomas Whiting, but the character depicted is certainly the latter.

Flora's connection with Buckingham has been recognised in the Old Gaol Museum. This is a fascinating building in its own right, built in 1748 in the style of a stone castle, with additions built in 1839, possibly designed by George Gilbert Scott. A unique permanent display about Flora opened on 25 May 2007 to celebrate the 60th anniversary of her death. The display, entitled *The Home of Flora Thompson*, includes the typewriter she used to type her books, with two life-size dioramas, one featuring Flora at home in Dartmouth in Devon, where she wrote *Lark Rise to Candleford*, and the other depicting a scene from her childhood in Juniper Hill, illustrating the life of the rural poor in the late 19th century. The museum has the only display of Flora memorabilia and exhibits some of its extensive collection of books by her and about her, together with related material such as the delicate Buckinghamshire lace, which was made in the local area (Flora wrote a vivid description of *Queenie* the lacemaker).The museum has a study centre, and is actively collecting material about Flora and acting as a centre for research. The staff have advised the BBC on their drama series based on *Lark Rise to Candleford*.

Ford Street with the tower and steeple of the parish church visible on the left. The church was rebuilt in the late 18th century after the tower of the medieval church fell down. It was built on top of the earthworks of the former castle, which is documented as having had a resident constable until at least 1599. The original castle may have been built in the time of Edward the Elder (899-924), who made Buckingham one of his twenty-five burhs or fortified towns. The castle probably housed the Anglo-Saxon mint established in the reign of Edgar (959-975), which continued until 1060. In 1975 there were only thirty-six recorded examples known world-wide of Anglo-Saxon coins minted in Buckingham, two-thirds of which were housed in museums on the continent.

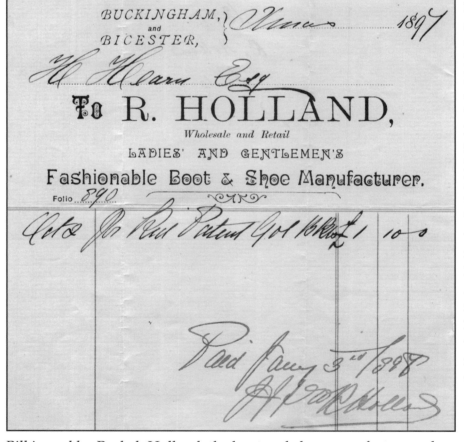

Bill issued by Rechab Holland, the boot and shoe manufacturer who may have been part of the inspiration behind Flora's *Uncle Tom,* though the main inspiration was her aunt's husband Thomas Whiting.

The Old Gaol, Buckingham

The *Old Gaol* built by Lord Cobham in 1748 on Market Hill in the form of a miniature castle. The semicircular south front (visible here) was added in 1839 to provide accommodation for the gaoler. It now houses a museum, which includes a gallery dedicated to the life and work of Flora Thompson.

Part of the Flora Thompson exhibition in the *Old Gaol Museum*. (Courtesy of the *Old Gaol Museum*)

The row of houses in Mitre Street where Flora's grandparents Thomas and Martha Timms lived in the 1870s.

Name.	Abode.	When buried.	Age.	By whom the Ceremony was performed.
Thomas Timms	The Workhouse Buckingham	Nov 10th	71.	J. Stewart Curate

BURIALS in the Parish of _Buckingham_
in the County of _Bucks_ in the Year 18_80_

No. 1609

Parish register entry recording the death of Thomas Timms in the Buckingham workhouse and his burial on 10 November 1880. (Courtesy of Revd Philip Derbyshire, Associate Priest in Buckingham Benefice)

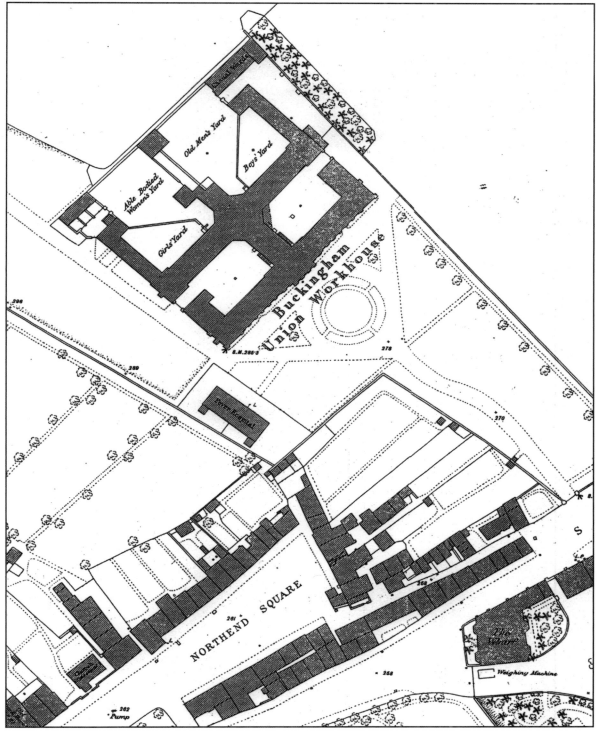

Ordnance Survey map surveyed in 1879 showing the Buckingham Union Workhouse near Northend Square, where Flora's grandfather Thomas Timms died in November 1880.

The house on Bristle Hill where stonemason John Waine died in 1930. In 1910 the house belonged to Earl Temple of Wotton. John Waine was the first cousin of Albert Timms, Flora's father, and may be the person on whom Flora Thompson partly based *James Dowland* in *Lark Rise to Candleford* and *Thomas Hearne*, the stonemason, in *Still Glides the Stream*. On John's death the front room of the property was found to be full of his carvings, particularly small animals.

Stonemason John Waine carved his wife's gravestone, on which his own details were added after his death. Here the white marble stone is seen in the 1960s in the town's civic cemetery, after it had been cleaned.

Flora's cousin Harry Wallington Waine (1878-1948) drove the shunting engine at Buckingham railway station for many years. He was the only son of John Waine the stonemason.

The railway station, Buckingham, with the Buckingham to Bletchley steam train standing at the platform. The photograph was taken by photographer James Venn at 4 p.m. on Saturday, 30 March 1957. (Courtesy of the Centre for Buckinghamshire Studies)

The Earl and Countess of Caithness with the Revd William Ross of Kintore on the front seat of the steam carriage built by Thomas Rickett at the Castle foundry in Buckingham. Rickett is seen on the rear platform. The photograph was taken on the occasion of the Earl's epic journey from Inverness to Barrogill Castle, a distance of some 150 miles, which began on 3 August 1860 and finished on 6 August. (Courtesy of Buckinghamshire County Museum)

BRACKLEY

It is very difficult to specify precisely the towns Flora used as her inspiration for the town of *Candleford*, as there are surprisingly few references to the town in *Lark Rise to Candleford* and many of these are vague, such as how wonderful it was to be able to pop out and buy a reel of thread or the miracle of finding fish displayed on a bed of reeds, sprinkled with ice, in the middle of summer. However, she must have often visited the small town of Brackley, as it was her nearest market town, even though it was over the county border in Northamptonshire. It was here that her father Albert Timms worked as a stonemason most of his life. Flora wrote that he worked for builders who had been based in Brackley for thirty five years, walking, or later cycling, the three miles there and three miles back, working from six in the morning until five in the afternoon, so that he often left home before daybreak.

Albert probably worked first for builder William Hawkins, the son of schoolmaster Thomas Hawkins. William was born in 1826 and was working as a painter in 1841, aged 15. Ten years later he was living in the High Street, working as a plumber, painter and glazier, with one employee. He had moved to St James by 1861 and employed five mechanics, an apprentice and three labourers. In 1871 he employed twenty-seven men and four boys. After he died in 1891, the business was taken over by his son William, who described himself as a builder and contractor.

Albert later worked for James Coles, who was born in Buckingham and first appears in Brackley records in the High Street in 1881 as a *'mantle mason, master employing two men'*. Ten year later he described himself as a *'stone and marble mason'*, with premises in the Banbury Road. In 1901 it had become a real family business, with three of his sons working with him. His house, with its carved stone plaque reading *The Statuaries* is still there, although his builder's yard behind it has now become a housing estate.

Another Brackley link with Albert Timms is found in the books of the Brackley-based *Rock of Hope Lodge* of the *IAAF Manchester Unity Friendly Society*. Albert Timms belonged to this and the secretary was a local builder, Alan Wootton. Albert would pay a regular sum to the Lodge every month and was entitled to receive sickness benefits and funeral expenses, a necessary insurance in the days before the National Health Service and Social Security. He was contracted to pay two shillings and sixpence per month, but the records reveal that sometimes his payments were irregular and he had to make up deficits later, which backs up Flora's comments about his attitude to money. The account book of the Lodge reveals that he received sick pay of two shillings with six pence for incidentals in March 1886, June 1887 and March and December 1888. When Flora wrote about Charity Finch's father visiting the

Oddfellows Benefit Club in *Mixlow* in *Still Glides the Stream,* she may have been thinking about her father's *Rock of Hope Lodge.* The members met for a convivial social evening each month, with refreshments and stimulating conversation.

Brackley is a small quiet town with an old-world feel and, although the shop fronts are different and there are more road markings, the basic layout of the long market place and the medieval planned borough is substantially the same as in Flora's time. It had a medieval castle along what is now the Hinton road. A station was opened for the LNWR Bletchley to Banbury railway in 1846-7 and another for the Great Central Leicester to Marylebone line in 1893. (Yet Flora wrote that when she visited Banbury as a child she went on the carrier's cart rather than by rail.)

Brewing was the main industry in the town Albert knew, as described in *Kelly's Directory of Northamptonshire* in 1890, but its rural character was emphasized by the presence of farmers, market gardeners and seedsmen, a higgler, the miller (who used water and steam power) and crafts which supplied rural and urban needs such as the harness maker, saddler, shoeing smith and wheelwright. A market was held each Wednesday, specialising in cattle and corn on alternate weeks, and a wool fair was held in June and a show of horses and agricultural products in September, with other fairs in October and December. Other crafts included wood turning and pillow-lace manufacture. The building trade was represented by builders, plasterers, masons, carpenters, plumber, house decorator, painter and gravestone cutter.

Flora Thompson would have been fascinated by the wide variety of shops, including the usual tailor, milliner, dressmaker, seamstress, draper, clothier, haberdasher, boot makers, butcher, baker, fishmonger, confectioner, commercial traveller, ironmonger, stationer and fancy repository, coal merchant, newsagent, tobacconist, beer retailer, publicans, house agent, Co-operative Society, chemist, chimney sweep and rope and twine maker. More unusual shops included the dealer in foreign postage stamps, the watch manufacturers, a marine store dealer, a coach builder and a photographer. There were several public houses.

Professional people included a medical officer and a doctor, veterinary surgeon, solicitors, surveyor and land agent, a registrar of births, marriages and deaths, the Bucks and Oxon Union Bank, Gillett's Bank and an accountant. There was a cottage hospital and a Union workhouse and a Magistrates' Court. News was provided by the *Brackley Observer,* which was published each Friday. Magdalen College School has been established in Brackley since the reign of Henry VIII, when students fled Oxford due to plague. In 1890 there was also a National School, a Wesleyan school and a ladies' school run by Miss Elizabeth Russell.

TOWN HALL, MARKET SQUARE, BRACKLEY.

An early postcard of the Market Place viewed from the south-west with, in the centre, the town hall built by the Duke of Bridgewater in 1706, which consists of a two storied structure with a hipped roof and cupola. On the right can be seen the white tiled front of premises which later became Thomas Waine's butcher's shop.

Thomas Charles Waine, a cousin of Flora Thompson, standing in the doorway of his butcher's shop in 1935.

Brackley market place with a wool fair in operation in 1900.

The Banbury Road, which runs off the southern end of Brackley's market place.

The former house, *The Statuaries,* and workshops belonging to James Coles's builder's yard in the Banbury Road near the Market Place road junction. Flora Thompson's father is believed to have worked here as a stonemason. (Courtesy of Martin Haslett)

The ornately carved signboard of *The Statuaries* located above the front bay window on the ground floor of the Banbury Road house front. (Courtesy of Martin Haslett)

Figure of a winged angel with the date 1884, split on either side of a potted rose on the first floor of *The Statuaries* overlooking the Banbury Road. Could the carving be the work of Albert Timms? (Courtesy of Martin Haslett)

1880 balance sheet for the *Loyal Rock of Hope Lodge*, Brackley branch of the *Independent Order of Oddfellows*, of which Flora's father Albert Timms was a member and which held meetings at the *Greyhound Inn*.

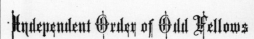

Independent Order of Odd Fellows　Manchester Unity Friendly Society,

LOYAL "ROCK OF HOPE" LODGE, NO. 3333,

(ESTABLISHED 1842.)

HELD AT THE "GREYHOUND" INN, BRACKLEY.

CAPITAL, £622 11S. 8½D.

BALANCE SHEET FOR THE YEAR ENDING DECEMBER 31, 1880.

SICK AND FUNERAL FUND.

DR. RECEIPTS.	£ s. d.	CR. PAYMENTS.	£ s. d.
To Capital of Sick and Funeral Fund Dec. 31st, 1880	594 13 4	By Members full Pay	101 8 4
„ Members' Contribution Cards	169 6 3½	„ Ditto (ditto)	26 0 0
„ Members of other Lodges	20 7 8½	„ Other ditto ditto	5 15 8
„ Proposition and Making	6 2 6	„ Funerals	35 0 0
„ Funeral Money from District	35 0 0	„ District Bill	27 14 6
„ Sick Pay returned from other Lodges	6 14 0	„ E. Bandy's Truss	0 12 6
„ Interest on Capital	16 1 0	„ Cash to other Lodges	15 16 6
		„ Other Members for Surgeons, to Incidental Fund	4 13 3½
			217 0 9½
		„ Balance of Sick and Funeral Fund	631 4 0½
	£848 4 10	Total	£848 4 10

MANAGEMENT FUND.

DR. RECEIPTS	£ s. d.	CR. PAYMENTS.	£ s. d.
To Contributions, own Members, to December 31st, 1880	32 10 7	By Balance due to Treasurer, December 31st, 1880	4 4 3½
„ Levies	7 18 8	„ Surgeon's Bill for One Year	35 0 0
„ Extra Funerals	8 7 6	„ Auditors	1 7 6
„ Other Members to Management	0 13 8	„ Delegates to District Meeting	2 0 0
„ Ditto Ditto to Surgeons	5 10 11	„ Secretary's Salary for one Year	8 19 0
„ Postage and Goods	0 14 3½	„ Stationery	0 11 0
„ Fines	0 8 9	„ Printing	1 1 6
„ Honorary Subscriptons	6 4 0	„ Goods and Postage	1 8 5
„ Balance	8 12 4	„ Rent of Lodge Room	2 10 0
		„ Extra Funerals	8 10 0
		„ District Bills	5 9 0
	£71 0 8½		£71 0 8½

BANBURY

Although Banbury was the furthest away of the towns Flora Thompson used as inspiration for her town of *Candleford*, she visited it several times as a child. She confirmed that she used Banbury as one of her influences in a letter written to her nephew Leslie Castle on 22 January 1945:

> *'Many thanks for your letter and the 'Hundred Years of Banbury', which is most interesting, I had no idea it had become to that extent an industrial town, or so large and thickly popu-lated. I knew it in my childhood as a very quiet country market town, as partly described in 'Over to Candleford', the other part being Buckingham.'*

She added more in a second letter written a month later on 24 February 1945:

> *'I was very interested in what you told me in your letter about Banbury. I had always thought of it in connection with the fighting in the Civil War and the Puritan hanging the cat on Monday for catching a mouse on Sunday and of Banbury Cross and, all the time, it has been growing into a large industrial town. I went there several times in the carrier's cart as a child and had that place partly in mind when creating my Candleford, though most of our relations lived in Buckingham. I must really try to see it once more after the war is over.'*

Banbury is the second-largest town in Oxfordshire and an important market town for the ten-mile area around it, locally known as *Banburyshire*. It had a population of 9660 in 1881. As well as being part of the inspiration for *Candleford*, it was, unusually, mentioned by name several times in Flora's novel *Still Glides the Stream*.

The town was much affected by the Civil War, because William Fiennes, Lord Saye and Sele of nearby Broughton Castle, who also owned Banbury Castle, was a noted Parliamentarian supporter and the town, strongly influenced by Puritanism, followed suit. In July 1642, before King Charles I had raised his standard at Nottingham, there was confrontation over six pieces of ordnance held at Banbury Castle. The first major battle of the Civil War, fought a few miles away at Edgehill on 23 October 1642, ended in stalemate, but three days later Banbury Castle surrendered to the King and was held for him by various members of the Compton family for the next three and a half years, making Banbury a Royalist strong-hold in a largely Parliamentarian area. There were attempts by Parliamentarians to retake the town in December 1642 and May 1643 and from July until late October 1644 the castle was besieged in vain, being relieved by a Royalist army under the Earl of Northampton. After that, the castle defences were strengthened and many buildings in the market place were destroyed to leave space between the town and the castle. A second siege took place in 1646 when the castle was undermanned and 19-year-old William Compton was in command. It surrendered and the defences were destroyed and the castle demolished, when the towns-people petitioned to be able to use its stone to rebuild their houses after the war.

Banbury was notoriously Puritan in the 17th century, encouraged by the preacher William Whateley, whose most famous sermon was entitled *Sinne no More!* Several people lampooned the town's zeal for Puritanism, including William Davenant who wrote in *The Wits*:

'That a weaver of Banbury, that hopes
To intice Heaven, by singing, to make him lord of twenty looms.'

Ben Jonson, the playwright, referred in *Bartholomew Fair* in 1614 to a Banbury baker en-titled *Zeal-of-the-Land Busy* (perhaps in real life the Banbury baker Richard Busby) who gave up making Banbury cakes because he was so horrified that they were served at pagan feasts such as bride ales, maypole and morris dancing, of which he violently disapproved. How-ever, Banbury cakes continued to be made and were a special delicacy enjoyed by Flora.

Banbury's cross has been made immortal by the rhyme:

Ride a cock horse to Banbury Cross,
To see a fine lady upon a white horse,
With rings on her fingers and bells on her toes,
She shall have music wherever she goes.

There were in fact several crosses in Banbury: the white cross, which was probably a boundary marker, the Bread Cross in Butcher's Row and the High Cross situated in Cornhill, to the north of the market place. The latter, which had steps up to a shaft decorated with sculptures, was demolished in 1601, allegedly because a certain John Trafford of Grimsbury venerated it, doffing his cap to it as he passed, which Puritans, including William Knight, considered was endangering his immortal soul. The inhabitants of Banbury were instructed by the court of Star Chamber to restore it, but nothing was done until the 19th century when the present cross was built in Horsefair (erroneously thought to be the original site) to com-memorate the marriage in 1858 of the Princess Royal, Victoria Adelaide Maria Louise, to Frederick William, Prince of Prussia.

Many of the agricultural machines, which Flora commented were taking over the jobs of the agricultural labourers and changing the face of the countryside, could have been man-ufactured in Banbury at Samuelsons. Bernhard Samuelson founded his Britannia Works in Fish Street in 1848, changing Banbury from a market town to an industrial centre. Although the firm suffered in the agricultural depression of the 1870s, it continued production until 1933. One of its famous products was the sail reaper, made under licence from McCormick. Samuelson was a benefactor to the town and encouraged adult education by setting up a Mechanics' Institute. This may be the inspiration for Flora's reference to one where she was able to borrow books.

An historical pageant commemorating the ride of a fine lady to Banbury Cross, assembled around the cross in the early 1900s. The cross was erected in Horsefair, erroneously thought in the 19th century to be the site of the medieval cross cited in the well-known nursery rhyme, though it was in fact situated in Cornhill, to the north of the Market Place. The Victorian cross was erected in 1858-9 to commemorate the marriage of the Princess Royal to the Crown Prince of Prussia and was designed in the style of an Eleanor Cross by Gibbs of Oxford. Figures of Queen Victoria, King Edward VII and King George V were added in 1914. In the background, on the right, can be seen the tower of St Mary's parish church.

St Mary's parish church, drawn by architect John Bloxham in 1975. It was built on the site of the 12th century church which was demolished in the late 18th century. A team of ten horses was used to pull down the west end and the spring of the wall was so strong that some of them were pulled up into the air during the demolition. The present building dates from 1790 and was designed by S. P. Cockerell. The parish ran out of money so the tower was not added until 1822, leading to the rhyme *'Dirty Banbury's proud people, built a church without a steeple.'*

Sinne no more,

OR

A SERMON PREACHED

in the Parish Church of *Banbury* on
Tuesday the fourth of March last past, vpon
occasion of a most terrible fire that happened there
on the Sabbath day immediately precedent, and within the
space of foure houres was carried from the one end of the
Towne to the other, with that fury, as continuing to burne
all the night, and much of the next day, it consumed
103 dwelling houses, 20 kilne-houses, and other
out-houses, to the number of 660 bayes and
vpwards, together with much malt and
other graine and commodities, as
amounted at the least to the
value of twenty thou-
sand pounds.

*The third time published and enlarged
by the Author,*

WILLIAM WHATELY, Vicar of *Banbury,*
2. PET. 3. 14.

*The heauens being on fire shall be dissolued,
and the element shall melt with feruent heat.*

LONDON.
Printed for *George Edwards* in *Greene Arbour*
without Newgate, 16⅞.

REPRINTED BY J. G. RUSHER,
BRIDGE-STREET, BANBURY,
MDCCCXXIV.

William Whately was one of the most famous of the Puritan divines. He was awarded his degree from Cambridge in 1604 and was Vicar of Banbury from 1610 until his death thirty years later. His vociferous preaching earned him the nickname of *'the roaring boy.'* His sermon *'Sinne no More'* preached after the Great Fire of Banbury, which destroyed one-third of the town in 1628, blamed the catastrophe on the sins of the townspeople. (Courtesy of Oxfordshire County Council Photographic Archive)

Parsons Street, which links the Horsefair to the Market Place, looking east. On the left stands the Reindeer Inn, dating back to the 16th century, where leading members of the Parliamentary army assembled to discuss strategy on the eve of the Battle of Edgehill. On the right, the building with the white front is the *Original Banbury Cake Shop* where Flora Thompson may have purchased Banbury cakes.

The interrogation of a Royalist by Parliamentarians in the Globe Room at the back of the Reindeer Inn. (Courtesy of Oxfordshire County Council Photographic Archive)

The Town Hall, Banbury Market Day.

Banbury Market Place on market day in c1905. In the centre stands the Town Hall, built in 1854 in Gothic style by E. Bruton. Additions were made in 1891.

Engineer Bernhard Samuelson moved to England in 1848 when his railway works in Tours (France) was closed due to the Revolution. He founded the Britannia Works in Fish Street manufacturing agricultural machinery, and succeeded in changing Banbury from a market town to an industrial centre. By 1860 the town was as famous for its agricultural implements as for its cross and its cakes. (Courtesy of Oxfordshire County Council Photographic Archive)

BIBLIOGRAPHY

Archer, Rowena	'Piety, Chivalry and Family: The Cartulary and Psalter of Sir Edmund Rede of Boarstall' (d.1489). Essay published in Soldiers, Nobles and Gentlemen, edited by Peter Coss and Christopher Tyerman, 2009
Aubrey-Fletcher, J.	Sir John Aubrey, Sixth Baronet of Llantrithyd, 1739-1826, 1988
Barrington, Peter	The Changing Faces of Bicester, Book One 1998
Barrington, Peter and Watts, David	The Changing Faces of Bicester Book Two, 1999
Blomfield, J.C.	History of the Present Deanery of Bicester, 8 volumes, 1882-94
Bloxham, Christine	The World of Flora Thompson, 1998
	The World of Flora Thompson Revisited, 2007
	May Day to Mummers, 2002
	Folklore of Oxfordshire, 2005
	The Book of Banbury, 1975
Booth, P., Evans, J. and Hiller, J.	Excavations in the Extra-Mural Settlement of Roman Alchester, Oxfordshire in 1991, 2002
Booy, David, ed.	The Selected Writings of Nehemiah Wallington, 2007
Carleton Williams, Ethel	Companion into Oxfordshire, 1935
Chandler, Keith	Morris Dancing in the English South Midlands, 1660-1900, 1993
	Ribbons, Bells and Squeaking Fiddles, 1993
	'Popular Culture in Microcosm: The Manuscript Diaries of Richard Heritage of Marsh Gibbon, Buckinghamshire', Folk Music Journal, Vol. IX, No. 1
	Musicians in 19th Century Southern England, n.d.
Costar, I, ed.	Ludgershall: A Village in Buckinghamshire, 2003
Delafield, John Ross	The History of the Delafield family, Vols. I and II, 1945
Drake-Brockman, Jennifer	'A Shropshire Poet in the Cotswolds', Country Life, 25.11.1976

Drinkwater, John   Inheritance, Being the First Book of an Autobiography, 1931.
                          Discovery, Being the Second book of an Autobiography, 1932.
Dunkin, John   History and Antiquities of Bicester, 1816
                          History and Antiquities of the Hundreds of Bullingdon and Plough-
                          ley, 1823, Vol. I and II
Elliott, Douglas J,   Buckingham, the Loyal and Ancient Borough, 1975
Farley, Michael   'A Medieval Pottery Industry at Boarstall, Buckinghamshire',
                          Records of Bucks, Vol. XXIV, 1982
Flaxman, Ted
and Joan   Cottisford Revisited, 1999
Fowler, J.K.   Echoes of Old Country Life, 1892
Gibbs, Robert   A Record of Local Occurrences in Buckinghamshire,
                          Vol. III, 1880
Goff, John   An Account of the Camfield Family of Northamptonshire, 1975

Greenwood, Martin   Fringford Through the Ages, 2000
                          Villages of Banburyshire: Including Lark Rise to Candleford, 2006
                          In Flora's Footsteps, 2009
Hawkes. H.W.   Sanderson Miller of Radway 1716-1780 (dissertation on the internet)
Hedges, Sid   Bicester wuz a Little Town, 1968
Henig, Martin and
Hornby, Simon   'A Cornelian Intaglio from Blackthorn Hill', Oxoniensia, Vol. LVI, 1991
Henig, Martin and
Booth, Paul   Roman Oxfordshire, 2000
Herring, Rowland   I Remember Blackthorn, 1998
Hinton, David   'Bicester Priory', Oxoniensia, Vol. XXXIII, 1968
                          'Excavation at Bicester Priory', Oxoniensia, Vol. XXXIV, 1969
Hudson, William   The Life and Legacy of James Goble of Worthing and Bicester, 2007
Kennett, White   Parochial Antiquities attempted in the History of Ambrosden,
                          Burcester and other adjacent parts ... , 1695
Lindsay, Gillian   The Story of the 'Lark Rise' Writer, 1990
Lipscomb, George   History and Antiquities of the County of Buckingham, Vol. I-IV, 1847
Lobel, Mary D., ed.   The Victoria History of the County of Oxford, Vol. VI, 1959
Lysons, Revd Daniel
and Lysons, Samuel   Magna Britannia, Bedfordshire, Berkshire and Buckinghamshire,
                          Vol. I, 1806
Marshall, R.M.   Oxfordshire Byways, 1935
Page, William, ed.   The Victoria History of the County of Buckingham Vol. IV, 1927

Payne-Galloway,
Sir Ralph   The Book of Duck Decoys, 1886
Prescott, Ann   Souldern: Our Village in Oxfordshire, 1994
Rahtz, Sebastian and
Rowley, Trevor   Middleton Stoney, 1984
Reed, Michael   The Buckinghamshire Landscape, 1979
Alfred Rimmer   Pleasant Spots around Oxford,1878
Sauer, Eberhard   'Alchester, Origins and Destiny of Oxfordshire's Earliest Site',
                     Oxoniensia, Vol. LXXI, 2006
Schultz, H.C.   'An Elizabethan Map of Wotton Underwood, Buckinghamshire', The
                     Huntington Library Quarterly, Vol III, No. I: October 1939
Seaver, Paul S.   Wallington's World: A Puritan Artisan in Seventeenth Century Lon-
                     don, 1985
Sergeant, John M.   The Story of Hethe, n.d.
Sherwood, Jennifer and
Pevsner, Nikolaus   The Buildings of England: Oxfordshire, 1974
Steane, John   The Northamptonshire Landscape, 1974
Thompson, Flora   Lark Rise to Candleford, 1971
                     Still Glides the Stream, 1948
                     Heatherley, 1998
                     The Peverel Papers, 1986
ed. Margaret Lane   The Country Calendar, 1979
Tucker, Pat   The Launton Lads Who Went to War, Launton Historical
                     Society, 1996
                     Let's Look at Launton, 1987
Warson, Gillian R.   Fact and Fiction: Flora Thompson and the Fewcott Part Book, 2003
Watts, David and
Barrington, Peter   The Changing Faces of Bicester Book, Three, 2000
                     The Changing Faces of Bicester Book, Four, 2001
                     The Changing Faces of Bicester Book, Five, 2003
Wing, William   Brief Annals of the Bicester Poor Law Union and its Component
                     Parishes in the Counties of Oxford and Buckingham, 1870

INDEX